1/18

ACCLAIM FOR THE FIRST EDITION

The Norwegian Lady
AND THE WRECK OF THE DICTATOR

"Foss not only tells the complete story of the *Dictator* for the first time, he has uncovered facts that are going to raise the eyebrows higher than the surf during a northeaster."

"It's one hell of story."

Lawrence Maddry
The Virginian-Pilot, Norfolk, Va.

"William O. Foss has done Virginia Beach a distinct favor in searching out both Hampton Roads and Norway in an effort to offer the first definitive account of The Norwegian Lady."

"*The Norwegian Lady and the Wreck of the Dictator* is a very welcomed addition to the archives of local history. It should not be relegated to the shelf, however, but should be read and passed on as a sea story we can all touch."

Metro Magazine, Norfolk, Va.

"The author lays to rest some ... legends but replaces them with true stories which enhance the image of the Captain's tragic figure."

"For history buffs, for admirers of the Norwegian Lady statue, for those with fondness for tales of the sea, *The Norwegian Lady and the Wreck of the Dictator* holds much of interest."

The Coastland Times, Manteo, N.C.

"The story of the wreck and how the Norwegian Lady became a link between Virginia Beach and a little-known town in Norway is told in this attractive local history."

U.S. Naval Institute Proceedings
Annapolis, Md.

"An interesting slice of local history linking Virginia Beach, USA, with Moss, Norway. Here is a fascinating tale of shipwreck, rescue, legend, tragedy and vindication."

The Seafarer, London, England

"Never before has the whole story been told, and through investigation by William O. Foss, who spent part of his youth in Norway ..., has uncovered little-known information about the aggrieved Captain Jorgensen, the details and aftermath of the shipwreck, and the dedication of American and Norwegian citizens to the creation of a tribute to all seafaring people."

Western Viking
Seattle, Wash.

"In this well written account, William Foss separates fact from fiction and presents a readable tale, in which the epilogue is just as interesting as the legends."

"Author Foss has done us a favor by writing this worthwhile story. The story of the Norwegian Lady is indeed compelling."

Vinland, Evanston, Ill.

The Norwegian Lady

AND THE WRECK OF THE DICTATOR

Other books by William O. Foss

Here is Your Hobby: Skiing
The United States Navy in Hampton Roads
It Happened First in Virginia
The Lives of Nine Cats
First Ladies Quotation Book

With Erik Bergaust

Coast Guard in Action
Helicopters in Action
Marine Corps in Action
Skin Divers in Action
Oceanographers in Action

The Norwegian Lady

AND THE WRECK OF THE DICTATOR

By William O. Foss

William O. Foss

The Norwegian bark Dictator, from a painting by an unknown artist. Photo courtesy of National Maritime Museum, London.

To
MY NORWEGIAN LADIES

Published by   Noreg Books
                  Post Office Box 66166
                  Virginia Beach, Virginia 23466-6166

First edition published in 1977
by The Donning Company, Publishers, Inc., Norfolk, Virginia.
Copyright © 1977 by William O. Foss

Revised edition. Copyright © 2002 by William O. Foss

Library of Congress Control Number: 2002092750
ISBN: 0-9721989-0-3

Cover by Wilma Fehrs-Foss

Printed in the United States of America.

CONTENTS

FOREWORD
TO THE FIRST EDITION

The lore of the sea, its ships and its men, the myths and facts, from Homer's Odyssey to the adventures of Jules Verne's Nautilus in Twenty Thousand Leagues Under the Sea, and the account of its modern counterpart, the atomic submarine Nautilus' expedition under the ice cap of the North Pole, has always fascinated man. But perhaps no period in time has captivated our imagination and intrigued us as much as the time of the "Tall Ships." The romance and drama of the high seas, the tales and recounts of adventure and bravery, the human triumphs and tragedies of these times, whether it be expeditions to and exploration of unknown parts of the world or the regular plying of trade around the globe—this is the material from which legends are made.

The story of the Norwegian bark Dictator and its captain, his family and his crew, though it might have gone down in the annals of the sea as just another shipwreck along the treacherous coast of the Atlantic, had in it the elements of such legends.

This book sorts fact from legend, and in the process may be said to kill one legend, but give birth to another. It is perhaps always a little sad to see a legend die, but the author's recount of a strong man's chance return to the place of his defeat and personal tragedy, there seizing a chance opportunity to "pay a debt" and, through sheer strength and courage, turning an impending tragedy into a human triumph by saving the lives of eight seemingly doomed men, thus replacing the myth with a no less romantic and inspiring reality, is certainly basis for another legend. And legendary Captain Jorgensen remains.

Because of these elements of human tragedy and triumph, facts and legend, the events off and on the beach of Virginia so many years back took hold of the minds and imaginations of the people involved and were passed on to new generations. Though the interest in the story has waxed and waned through the years, it never quite lost hold, perhaps in part thanks to the original "Norwegian Lady," the carved figurehead in the shape of a buxom lady that drifted onto the beach from the wreck of the Dictator, and which the people of Virginia Beach erected on their beach in memory of the people lost from that ill-fated ship.

These events so many years ago led to some remarkable events many years later, tying the people of two continents closer together. The small town of Moss in Norway and the city of Virginia Beach in the United States have become sister cities because of "The Norwegian Lady." And two beautiful statues, the new Norwegian Ladies, placed in those cities, stand looking out to sea on each side of the Atlantic as symbols of friendship between our peoples, and in memory of all valiant men lost at sea.

It is indeed a compelling story.

Harald Svanoe Midttun
Counselor
Press and Cultural Affairs
Royal Embassy of Norway,
Washington D.C.
25 March 1977

FOREWORD
TO THE REVISED EDITION

It is a distinct honor to add my words to those of Harald Svanoe Midttum in this foreword to *The Norwegian Lady and the Wreck of the Dictator*. It has been well over a hundred years since the Dictator wrecked on the sands of Virginia Beach and of the hundreds of shipwrecks that occurred along our shores, the Dictator is certainly the most remembered and the one which has made the most impact on our city. Even today the Dictator brings together the people of two nations to commemorate the loss of life as well as the heroic actions of the United States Life-Saving Service.

I wish to commend my friend Bill Foss for his thorough research and accurate accounting of the events surrounding the disaster. The results of his labor is a volume which stands out as a meaningful part of the maritime heritage of the City of Virginia Beach.

Today, the Old Coast Guard Station keeps the tradition of the United States Life-Saving Service alive, and relates the story of the wreck of the Dictator through a permanent exhibit. We are proud to stand shoulder to shoulder with Bill Foss in telling this story of tragedy and heroism.

Fielding Lewis Tyler
Executive Director
The Old Coast Guard Station
Virginia Beach, Virginia
16 May 2002

PREFACE

As a recent citizen of Virginia Beach I quickly became impressed with the magnificent statue of the Norwegian Lady facing the Atlantic Ocean from her pedestal at the oceanfront and Twenty-Fifth Street. The fact that my parents were Norwegians and that I spent my formative years in Norway probably enhanced my interest and curiosity about the real story of the Norwegian Lady. Why is she keeping her lonely vigil at the beach?

Since I was a boy in the town of Hyggen on the Drammensfjord in Norway I have been fascinated with the dramatic sagas of the seas. The Norwegian Lady has a tale to tell, but the inscription on the statue does not reveal the whole story.

I read with interest local newspaper accounts that appeared during the annual memorial to those who lost their lives in the wreck of the Norwegian bark Dictator off Virginia Beach on March 27, 1891, and how the legend of her master led to the erection of the Norwegian Lady statue.

The storytellers spun a melancholy tale, but they left some pertinent questions unanswered: Who was Captain Jorgensen? How could Captain Jorgensen have managed to arrange (let alone afford the expense) to return to Virginia Beach year after year to pay homage to his lost family? How strange it was that local storytellers seldom mentioned the names of those involved in the Dictator rescue operations! And who was the Norwegian Lady?

My search for the answers to these questions brought me in contact with many persons in the Tidewater Virginia area as well as in Norway, Canada, and England. Many of the people I contacted became caught up in the story and went to great lengths to provide me with valuable information. As far as shipwrecks go, the Dictator disaster was not a major tragedy, but the legend that arose from this sad event was of great significance, leading to a closer bond between the people of two distant cities, Virginia Beach in the United States and Moss in Norway.

Elsewhere I am acknowledging my sources and major contributors of historical data, but I would be remiss if I did not give special thanks to the following persons who provided me with indispensable information:

Finn Krogsrud of Kragero, Norway, who provided photographs and details on the life of Captain Jorgen M. Jorgensen and his wife Johanne Pauline.

Vernon Drinkwater, Sr., of Virginia Beach, who gave me interesting facts about his grandfather, Edward Drinkwater, Keeper of the Seatack Life Saving Station.

Miss Cornelia R. Holland of Virginia Beach, who contributed valuable historical photographs and anecdotes about early life in Virginia Beach.

Thomas Goode Baptist of Arlington, who recalled the events which led to the erection of the Norwegian Lady statue at Virginia Beach.

A word about literary license. When historical characters speak, their spoken words are based on actual statements made in official reports and in correspondence, or from direct quotes and attributions made in newspaper articles.

William O. Foss
Virginia Beach, Virginia
U.SA.
March 1977

CHAPTER ONE

STORMY GOOD FRIDAY

The morning of Good Friday, March 27, 1891, greeted early risers in Virginia Beach, Virginia, with torrential rains and strong east northeast winds whipping ocean salt spray and sands about the beach area. Wind velocity of up to fifty-four miles per hour was recorded by the Weather Bureau Station located at the site of the Cape Henry Lighthouse. Angry waves of the Atlantic Ocean slammed forcefully against the shore, shifting the sands and washing the pebbles and rocks.

At the Princess Anne Hotel, located on the oceanfront between what are now Fourteenth and Sixteenth Streets, S.E. Crittenden, the manager, fretted over what effect the inclement weather conditions would have upon new guests at the hotel. The shingle-structured hotel, with lookout towers from which its guests could observe ships sailing on the Atlantic Ocean, and wide verandas from which guests could observe swimmers and beach activities, was rapidly gaining popularity as a new resort spot for the genteel. The hotel's 139 rooms were nearly filled with guests, mostly repeaters from the New England states, who had discovered that one need not travel further south than Tidewater Virginia to enjoy an unmatchable combination of pleasant weather and pleasant living.

Spring comes early to Virginia Beach, and the Princess Anne Hotel guests were prepared to enjoy an Easter holiday filled with warm ocean breezes spawned by the passing Gulf Stream and inflowing tropical air masses. Those guests who were tired of northern snow and icicles could look forward to seeing a parade of spirit-lifting spring blossoms: dogwood, laurel, azalea, and flamboyant rhododendron.

If the dismal weather had a deterring affect upon the holiday spirit of any of the Princess Anne Hotel guests, it was not noticeable in seventeen-year-old Emily Gregory who, with her parents, Mr. and Mrs. David Gregory of Cooperstown, New York, were making their first visit to Virginia Beach. Peering through her bedroom window, Emily watched in awe and fascination as powerful white-foamed waves broke thunderously over the beach.

David Gregory, a lawyer practicing in New York City, had been urged by Crittenden to forego his usual Easter vacation in Florida for a new and exciting experience in Virginia Beach.

Emily, a tall and comely girl, thoroughly enjoyed herself, walking, running, skipping up and down the beach and on the sand dunes, sometimes alone, sometimes with new-found friends. She took particular delight in observing the graceful flights of the seagulls as they rode the crest of the waves searching for food. And she was amused by the quick movements and pitter-patter runs of the sandpipers scurrying along the beach in unison with the ebb and flow of the waves.

Among Emily Gregory's new Virginia Beach friends were Bernard P. Holland, an agent for the Norfolk, Albemarle and Atlantic Railroad, which ran a narrow gauge railroad from Norfolk to the Princess Anne Hotel. Holland, who shared a third-floor room with the hotel's clerk, also worked as an assistant hotel clerk during the evenings. He met Emily soon after the Gregory family arrived for their three-week vacation.

While it was love at first sight, Emily's parents insisted she become of age before marrying. Bernard and Emily were married four years later. An ambitious and enterprising man, Holland was destined to become Virginia Beach's first postmaster and mayor.

A little north of the Princess Anne Hotel, on a site at what is now Atlantic Avenue, between Twenty-fourth and Twenty-Fifth Streets, Captain Edward Drinkwater, keeper of the Seatack Life Saving Station, was having his morning coffee while receiving reports on the surf and beach conditions from wet and chilled Surfmen Stone and James A. Johnston, who had just come off the four a.m.-to-sunrise beach patrol.

Stone had walked the beach northward to a point where he met a surfman from the Cape Henry Life Saving Station, while Johnston had patrolled southward until he met the Dam Neck Mills surfman walking northward. They exchanged badges and returned to their own life saving stations, notifying their respective keepers of the situation in their particular patrol area. None had seen any signs of shipping off the beach.

Drinkwater wrote in his log that the wind direction was east-northeast and that the force of the wind was "strong." The state of the weather was "rainy" and the surf was "rough."

Other members of the Seatack Life Saving Station crew were Surfmen Creekmore, O' Neal, Jimmy Herrick, J. W. Robinson, John S. Sparrow, and James Burlas. Albert L Barco was absent because one of his brothers was very sick

The life saving crew, comprised of strong, courageous men who made their living as fishermen and sailors, were always ready for action, especially on a day such as this. They were trained to perform their duties in bad weather; shipwrecks and marine accidents seldom occur under sunny skies and on calm seas. On this Good Friday morning, they seemed to be taking unusual care in making their routine check of life saving equipment.

The compact, two-story life saving station building, of pointed architecture, was built in 1879 as Station Number Two in a chain of

Seatack Life Saving Station. Photo courtesy of Miss Cornelia R. Holland, Virginia Beach, Virginia

coastal rescue stations that the United States Life Saving Service operated in its Sixth District, which had jurisdiction over life saving stations in Virginia and North Carolina.

Station Number One was located three-quarters of a mile southeast of the Cape Henry Lighthouse, while the Seatack station was five miles south of the Cape Henry light. Four miles farther south was the Dam Neck Mills Life Saving Station.

Crewman at a United States Life Saving Station fakes the messenger line of the Lyle cannon line throwing gun. It will be stored in the peg box to be ready for the next drill exercises or for an actual shore-to-ship breeches buoy rescue. The station's horse earns his oats, in the background, after pulling the lifeboat wagon and breeches buoy carriages, all in a day's work. United States Coast Guard photo taken before 1915.

Two additional life saving stations were located on the Virginia coast: Little Island Life Saving Station on the beach abreast of North Bay and the False Cape Station on the beach abreast of Back Bay.

Seatack was the name given by the community to that part of the beach where the British landed an amphibious force during the War of 1812. Over the years the local people changed the area name from "Sea Attack" to "Sea Tack" and eventually combined into one word, "Seatack."

The first floor of the life saving station contained a large boatroom, where a variety of rescue apparatus was stored, including a lifeboat, a beach cart, Coston lights, the Lyle gun—a cannon-type line throwing gun-and breeches buoys. The station had also a life car, a short, flat torpedo-like container built of corrugated iron, which held six to eight passengers and was used to rescue persons from stricken vessels by hauling them through the water rather than by an aerial line, as in the case of the breeches buoy.

Crew of a United States Life Saving Station launchng a surfboat to assist a grounded ship in the background, circa 1880. United States Coast Guard photo.

A living room for the crew was located on the first floor of the station, while a small sleeping room was located on the second floor. A small room, where the keeper kept his log books, official papers, and communication equipment, was also located on the second floor. The station house had space for up to twenty-five persons and was kept supplied with provisions to feed that number of shipwreck survivors for ten days.

An open lookout deck, from which the life saving station crew could scan the ocean in all directions, was located on top of the building.

While the life saving station was furnished with utensils for cooking, the crew had to purchase their own provisions out of their ten dollars weekly pay. Drinkwater, as the keeper, received an annual salary of seven hundred dollars.

At nine o'clock in the morning, Edward Drinkwater received a telephone call from Captain Bailey Barco, keeper of the Dam Neck Mills Life Saving Station, advising him that a sailing ship was spotted about a mile from the beach, standing to the northward, close-hauled on the starboard tack, and under shortened canvas.

"She looks to be in trouble," said Barco, "so you'd better keep a sharp lookout for her." Barco noted that the vessel was laboring, pitching and rolling heavily in the turbulent sea.

Captain Drinkwater immediately ordered one of the surfmen to watch the ocean for any sign of the vessel from the observation platform atop the station house. Other crewmen rechecked rescue apparatus that might be used in the event of trouble.

About ten o'clock the Seatack Life Saving Station lookout, peering into the hard-driven rain and mist, spotted the sailing vessel passing north of the station close to shore. A few minutes later, she was observed by the station crew to square away before the wind toward the beach. She was then a little less than a mile north of the station, near where Fortieth Street now runs into the oceanfront.

Keeper Drinkwater ordered his men into action.

"Break out your buoy apparatus and move out!" he commanded.

The men donned their foul-weather clothing, ran out the breeches buoy equipment, and started toward the vessel. Since the high tide made the beach area impassable, some of the surfmen moved their life saving equipment on a byway behind the sand hills in a cart hauled by a pair of mules owned by John G. James. Others kept to the beach in company of a party of fishermen from a fishing camp near the station.

Before departing his station, Captain Drinkwater telephoned Captain Odward W. Johnston, keeper of the Cape Henry Life Saving Station, suggesting that the Cape Henry crew come and aid the three-master that was in trouble off shore.

"We'll move out right away," replied Johnston. ·

Drinkwater also telephoned Barco at Dam Neck Mills to advise that the bark was coming ashore.

The Seatack life saving crew reached the area where the troubled ship was fighting to keep away from the shore about 10:45 in the morning.

As the surfmen and fishermen looked out toward the distressed ship, she suddenly turned head on toward the beach.

"She's struck!" someone yelled.

The people on the beach saw the stricken ship shudder as she hit the outer edge of a sand bar, about 350 yards from the shore.

"I wonder who she is," a surfman said as he readied the rescue equipment.

Chapter Two

THE DICTATOR

The ship was the Norwegian-owned bark Dictator whose master, Captain Jorgen Martinius Jorgensen, and crew were exerting all their energies and knowledge of seamanship to keep her away from the treacherous Virginia shore. But the aged three-master, off course and already weakened by earlier storms, was unable to keep seaward against the buffeting winds and battering waves.

An inglorious and sad end was about to befall this once proud and beautiful vessel, whose crews and masters had sailed her to the world's greatest trading centers from Constantinople to Singapore. She had conquered fog and ice in the North Atlantic Ocean, fought the violent seas around Cape Horn, and had weathered monsoons in the Indian Ocean.

The Dictator first hit the waters in May 1867, not as a bark, but as a full-rigged ship, built by John Nevins in his yard near Rankine's wharf, Saint John, New Brunswick, Canada. The ship, of 1,293 register tons, then christened the Connemara, was owned by Wm. P. Sinclair & Co., of Liverpool, England. The length of the Connemara was 191.4 feet, breadth was 37.7 feet, and depth of hold was 23.1 feet. A beautiful, hand-carved figurehead of a buxom Victorian looking lady adorned her bow. Her master was Captain J. Hughes, and the destination of her first voyage was India.

In 1874 the Connemara was altered to include a poop, a deck above the stern of the ship.

Hadden & Wainwright, also of Liverpool, purchased the Connemara in 1879.

In 1884, Christian Monrad Holst, a shipowner and an assistant bank chief in the Moss Savings Bank in Moss, Norway, decided to purchase the Connemara for his family-owned shipping line.

Ring life preserver from the Norwegian bark Dictator. Close examination reveals the ship's first name, Connemara, and her homeport, Liverpool. Photo by William O. Foss.

By now the hard-driven Connemara was beginning to show her age; the strain and stresses she suffered in her many deep sea voyages had weakened her masts, yards, and hull.

Holst, who had taken over the shipping line after the death of his father, Fredrik J. Holst, was optimistic about plans for his new ship. He had her repaired, caulked her bottom, and re-entered her in the shipping trade as a bark, a three-masted ship with foremast and mainmast square-rigged and mizzenmast fore-and-aft rigged. The new entry in the Norwegian merchant fleet was rechristened Dictator.

Captain Andreas Theileman was named master of the Dictator, and he remained so until 1890 when he became ill during a call to Constantinople (now Istanbul). The first mate Johan Anton Mathisen sailed the ship back to Norway.

When Holst picked a new master for the Dictator, he sought an experienced sailor who was familiar with international trade. Many Norwegian seamen met these requirements, but Holst found his new skipper in thirty-one year old Jorgen Martinius Jorgensen who, ever since he was a teenager on the island of Skaatoy near the city of Kragero, had sailed on many ships that plied the trade routes. In the

1880s Jorgensen had been master of ships that sailed on Australian trade routes for the Kragero firm of A. F. Schroeder.

Tall and robust, Jorgensen was a strong-minded man who had a reputation of being loyal to his employers and determined and efficient in carrying out his job. A serious man, his short haircut and neatly-trimmed mustache emphasized his usual stern and prominent bearing.

Skaatoy, located about one and a half nautical miles from Kragero, is one of the larger of many islands—the Skerries—which rim the city and protect it against storms in the Skagerrak arm of the North Sea. A beautiful island, Skaatoy was then and is today inhabited by families who earn their livelihood as fishermen and sailors. Since this northern climate is tempered by the warm Gulf Stream, the area is also conducive to light farming and forestry.

Because of the many islands, some of them bare rocks and uninhabited except for seabirds and seals, navigation in these waters is extremely hazardous, and since the only means of getting anywhere was by boat, Jorgensen had learned the rudiments of navigation at an early age.

Jorgensen's home on Skaatoy was on the farmstead Donneviken—named after the nearby Donneviken bay. A short distance away was the farmstead Stoppedalen, owned by Knut Nilsen and his wife Johanne. Their attractive daughter Johanne Pauline, nicknamed "Paua," was a childhood sweetheart of Jorgensen.

After her marriage to Jorgensen, Johanne often sailed with her husband. It was not uncommon for Norwegian sea captains to take their wives and families with them on long voyages, and living with the sea all around her on Skaatoy, Johanne had no qualms about exchanging the comforts of a home on land for cramped quarters in a sailing vessel.

July 20, 1887, was an important day in the life of the Jorgensens. Johanne, then twenty-six years old, gave birth to a son. The birth took place far away from Norway, in Wellington, New Zealand. The proud parents named their son Carl and gave him the middle name of Zealand, in honor of the country of his birth.

When Jorgen Jorgensen became master of the Dictator, Johanne decided that she and Carl would sail with him. Jorgensen had suggested that it would perhaps be best for her to remain on Skaatoy where she and Carl could enjoy a more comfortable life.

"The sea is no place to rear a child," said Jorgensen.

"Don't fret about it, my dear," replied his personable wife. "I love

Captain Jorgen M. Jorgensen. Photo courtesy of Finn Krogsrud, Kragero, Norway.

Mrs. Johanne Pauline Jorgensen. Photo courtesy of Finn Krogsrud, Kragero, Norway.

Carl Zealand Jorgensen. Photo courtesy of Finn Krogsrud, Kragero, Norway.

you, and Carl and I want to be with you as long and as often as we can. We'll go home when the time comes for our son to attend school."

"But that won't be until he is six.

"Time goes fast when we are together." Jorgensen agreed reluctantly.

"We won't get in your way," she assured him.

On March 3, 1891, the Dictator left Pensacola, Florida, heavily loaded with a full cargo of yellow pine timber. Heading out into the Gulf of Mexico, with her draft being nearly twenty-three feet, the Dictator's destination was West Hartlepool, England.

The Jorgensens and the crew looked forward to this voyage, because once the timber was unloaded at West Hartlepool, the Dictator would return to her homeport in Moss.

While Johanne was adventurous and willing to live the arduous life of the sea, she longed to be home in May to enjoy the lovely Norwegian spring. There would still be patches of snow in the woods behind Kragero, but on Skaatoy and the other islands the sun would beckon for spring flowers, such as blue anemone and lily of the valley, to show their beauty. And if you listened carefully, in the distance you could hear the cuckoo bird make his pronouncement that spring had arrived.

After rounding the Florida Keys on March 12 the Dictator ran into a severe storm that pounded her fiercely. She lumbered heavily through the rough seas.

When the Dictator passed the Grand Bahama Island on March 19 on a course that would take her north of Bermuda, from which point she would follow the trade routes north-eastward to England, she was again hit by a tremendous tropical storm.

Riding low in the water because of her heavy load of pine, the Dictator became an easy prey for the big foaming waves which crashed over her deck, breaking asunder her guardrail. As the ship pitched and rolled heavily, the high waves smashed two of her lifeboats and swept them away from the davits into the raging sea.

As if this wasn't enough damage, the aging sailing vessel sprung a leak. The crew manned the steam pumps, but they had also been broken by the storm.

The Dictator was in grave trouble, but Captain Jorgensen, who had experienced danger before, ordered the crew to repair the pumps, and when that was not possible, to work the pumps manually. He was anxious to get to West Hartlepool on time.

But the weather was against the Dictator and every ship that sailed in the South Atlantic at this time. Nature seemed to have unleashed her most violent anger as storm upon storm raked the coastline from Florida to New Jersey. On the twenty-third of March a hurricane at Bermuda, with fierce squalls, lightning, and rain, moved toward the United States into the path of the luckless Dictator.

The Norwegian sailing ship, groaning and straining as powerful waves struck against her weakened hull, fought valiantly against the elements. The crew worked the pumps, but they could not stem the flow of water coming into the leaking bark. Some of the crew were becoming concerned over their safety.

On March 23, the Dictator experienced another harrowing period of stormy weather. Hurricane-force winds and furious waves spent their violence against the already battered and beaten vessel.

The constant punishment the ship had suffered since sailing through the Straits of Florida had an adverse affect not only on the aging sailing ship, but also on the weary crew. Water was now coming into the ship at the rate of two inches per hour, and the tired and disgruntled crew felt they were fighting a losing battle.

The first mate, Cornelius Nilsen, confronted Captain Jorgensen with a new problem.

"Sir, we can't stop the leaks, and the men are tired from working the pumps. They want you to change course for a safe port in America."

Jorgensen, who had been on the quarterdeck with little sleep since the storms first hit the vessel, said he was aware that everyone was tired, and suggested that repairs could be made once the storms subsided.

"Captain, I must warn you that things are quite serious," said Nilsen. "This old ship is hurt badly, and I doubt we can make it safely to England without repairs."

"I am aware of the damage—and the danger," replied the ship's master.

"There are murmurings amongst the crew," said the first mate. "Some of the men are refusing to work unless you go in for repairs."

Jorgensen frowned. He pondered his problem. He wanted desperately to get to West Hartlepool and then to Norway where he would tell Johanne that she and the boy must stay ashore. This series of seemingly unnatural storms had convinced him that the sea was no place for a family to live, no matter how much he wanted them with him. Johanne would be angry at first, but she would get over it soon.

The Dictator probably resembled this unidentified grounded three-masted schooner, here under investigation by a lifeboat crew from the Cape Henry Life Saving Station in the 1890s. From a glass negative of the United States Life Saving Service, courtesy of the Smithsonian Institution.

Living with their families, who loved her and the child, and being with friends on the islands and in Kragero, would make her content, he reasoned.

"Mister Nilsen, tell the men we are going into Hampton Roads in Virginia for repairs. We should find good repair facilities in Norfolk."

Captain Jorgensen's decision to seek repairs was greeted with enthusiasm by the crew, and Johanne, who had felt the tension of hostility build up among the crew, was much relieved when he told her of his command. She felt that some of the men resented her being aboard the ship; many seamen believe that to let a woman come aboard ship brings bad luck.

There were still the elements to fight. The storm that was pounding the Dictator was also endangering other ships off the Atlantic seaboard. Some succumbed to the overpowering wind and seas. On March 24, the steamship Strathairly was driven ashore and smashed to pieces one-and-a-quarter miles south of the Chicamicomico Life Saving Station,

North Carolina, with the loss of nineteen persons; seven were saved. Three days later, another steamship, the Bovinqueen, went ashore five miles south of Hatteras Inlet; fortunately her crew was saved.

On the morning of March 27 the bark Dictator approached the entrance to Chesapeake Bay. The weather was rainy and thick, the seas tumultuous, and strong winds ripped into the rigging. Captain Jorgensen, sailing cautiously and by dead reckoning, for he had been days without an observation of the sun, thought he was in the vicinity of the Cape Charles lightship. Unknown to Jorgensen, his ship was not near Cape Charles, but twenty-two miles farther south, in the vicinity of False Cape.

The leadsman, standing in the chains on the fo'c'sle, heaved the lead line to take soundings and guide the ship through the unknown waters.

"By the deep ten, Sir!"

"By the deep six, Sir!"

"Quarter less six, Sir!"

Suddenly the leadsman shouted through the roaring wind: "And a half four, Sir!", announcing that there were no more than four-and-a-half fathoms of water under the ship's keel.

Seeing broken water to the windward, or eastward, of the ship, Jorgensen tried to keep the Dictator off a couple of points, hoping to keep her in deep waters.

Instead of deepening water, however, the next thing he saw was a line of shore breakers close under his lee, and before the mistake could be corrected the Dictator's keel grated on the bottom.

Realizing that there was no way to escape, Jorgensen kept the ship headed directly for land, trying to get her as close as possible to the beach.

The Dictator quivered visibly; a moment later she came to a standstill solidly on the outer edge of the sandbar, about 350 yards from the shore.

An anguished silence fell over the ship.

CHAPTER THREE

THE RESCUE

Captain Jorgensen broke the silence when he shouted: "Cut away the mainmast!" He hoped to relieve the ship of her heavy topside burden, making it easier to fight the raging sea.

A seaman swung an axe and severed the lanyards of the weather rigging. Abetted by the strong wind, the mainmast snapped off just above the deck, taking the fore and mizzen topmasts with it as it fell. The masts, their rigging, and sails crushed the Dictator's two remaining lifeboats as they fell across the deck and over the side. Only a small, sixteen foot sharp-stern clinker-built boat was left intact.

Jorgensen went to his cabin, where his wife was trying to comfort their frightened and crying son. He embraced them both.

"Oh, Jorgen—God help us!"

"We are hard aground, but we are not too far from the shore. Don't be afraid. Rescue is near," he assured Johanne.

He directed his wife to put on one of his suits, explaining that her own clothing would be cumbersome on the wet and slippery rolling deck. Jorgensen also feared that his wife's lengthy and flowing clothing might get entangled in the ship's gear or make it difficult for her to move about in the event she had to attempt to swim ashore.

"Stay here in the cabin. You'll be safer here," he assured her. "I must see what can be done to get us ashore safely."

The Seatack Life Saving crew, struggling to make haste in the soft and wet sand, arrived at the scene about 10:45 in the morning and immediately laid out their life saving equipment: the Lyle cannon type line-throwing gun and projectiles, the messenger line and faking box, blocks, pulleys, and supporting boards for the hawser, and the breeches buoy, a life ring to which a pair of heavy canvas breeches were strongly attached.

Within five minutes the surfmen were ready to fire the line toward the distressed ship, but Captain Drinkwater delayed giving the order because he wanted to make certain that he had a sure shot.

The strong wind was blowing directly against the beach, and any shot would go dead into the eye of the wind. Furthermore, the stricken ship was nearly 350 yards away from the rescuers, and while the Lyle gun had a range of about five hundred yards, it was seldom used for more than 250 yards. For distances greater than 250 yards it was extremely difficult for sailors aboard distressed ships to pull the heavy rescue gear through the surf; during cold and stormy weather, such as was encountered at Virginia Beach, few men could stand being exposed to the elements and ride more than 250 yards through the pounding surf.

When Drinkwater ordered the Lyle gun to be fired, a number seven line was attached to the projectile. Fired directly into the eye of the wind, the projectile whizzed toward the bark. It fell short about forty yards.

A number four line—the smallest used—was faked out and tied to the projectile, but this shot was equally unsuccessful.

Meanwhile, the Cape Henry Life Saving Station crew, led by keeper Odward Johnston, had arrived at the rescue scene and began cooperating with the Seatack lifesavers.

Also arriving on the scene were S.E. Crittenden, manager of the Princess Anne Hotel, many of his hotel guests, numerous local fishermen, and conductors from the Norfolk, Albemarle and Atlantic Railroad.

The hotel visitors, most of them unaccustomed to the brutality that nature can inflict upon men who make their living by the sea, were both thrilled and horrified by the drama of seeing a ship being destroyed and human beings suffering possible death before their eyes. Some cried, others offered prayers, but most guests stood silently on the beach watching the struggle of life and death.

At noon, as keepers Drinkwater and Johnston were consulting on what their next move should be, an empty water barrel with a line attached to it was observed being dropped over the side by sailors onboard the Dictator. As the barrel drifted in toward the beach, Drinkwater ordered a line be fired over it, but the strong wind prevented the projectile from reaching its goal. The second shot, however, was successful, and at that very moment, an unusually heavy surge of seas brought the barrel within reach of the surfmen, who quickly tied the two lines together.

Drawing showing crews of the United States Life Saving Service using the breeches buoy to rescue persons from a stricken vessel. Photo from Records of the Life Saving Service, National Archives and Records Service.

The sailors began hauling the lines toward the ship. They fastened the tail block of the whip (a continuous line that goes through a pulley) to one of the starboard mizzen shrouds, just below the crosstrees, and the hawser (a heavy line which supports the breeches buoy) to the masthead above the eyes of the rigging.

But on the shore the life saving crews had trouble keeping the hawser line taut over the X-shaped crotch and also in securing the hawser to the buried wooden sand anchor. As the surf pushed the Dictator closer in, her stern swung shoreward, and the slackened hawser, which lay in the water, was being moved northward by the strong current. Only with the aid of the crowd of bystanders on the sand hills were the life saving crews able to take up the slack and fasten the hawser to the sand anchor.

THE BREECHES BUOY.

Shipwrecked sailor in a breeches buoy. This was one of a series of sketches on the United States Life Saving Service (forerunner of the United States Coast Guard) by M.J. Burnes, circa 1879, published in the old Harper's Weeklies. United States Coast Guard photo.

The lines connecting the ship with the shore party became so badly twisted while running through the surf that the sailors on the bark had to cut the bight of the whip at the block, take out the turns, and rejoin the ends by a long splice.

The breeches buoy, hung from a traveler block run on the hawser, was finally hauled to the bark by the whip. When the breeches buoy arrived on board ship, the lines were again badly twisted, but by applying brute force, the men were able to pull the lines through the block

Captain Jorgensen picked Seaman Jakob Mell to be the first man to board the breeches buoy. On a signal from the captain, the rescue party began hauling him ashore.

As the seaman was being pulled to shore on the breeches buoy, the pounding sea shifted the Dictator so that she was nearly in a parallel position to the shore. The bark now began rolling from side to side like a pendulum. When oscillating away from the beach, the line would suddenly tighten and swing the breeches buoy and the sailor high into the air. When the vessel rolled shoreward the line went slack, and the unfortunate Mell was dipped into the freezing surf. The surfmen and their helpers tried to keep the hauling line taut, but they couldn't cope with the rolling action of the ship.

Seaman Mell had been pulled about a third of the way to shore when the hauling or shore end of the whip broke. It had chafed and parted close to the buoy. This startling mishap was instantly discovered by Keeper Johnston, who was in charge of that part of the whip. Johnston ordered the surfmen to haul quickly on the other end of the whip, and Mell, half drowned and nearly unconscious, was pulled through the surf back to the ship.

The failure of the breeches buoy was a bitter disappointment to the Dictator crew, and while Captain Jorgensen now realized that the buoy could not be used, he calmly ordered the ship's only remaining small boat to be launched. Four men were told to get into the boat.

The launching was made under the most difficult circumstances — the wind was blowing furiously, the air was thick with blinding rain, and rushing water was breaking over the ship's deck as the bark rolled from the impact of the pounding waves.

Yet, by superb seamanship, the Dictator's sailors were able to secure the hoisting out tackles and lower the boat into the water. It was about one o'clock in the afternoon.

Jorgensen had a line tied to the small boat, thus enabling the boat to be slacked in to shore. He instructed the four sailors that if they reached the shore safely they were to find out whether the shore party was planning to launch a lifeboat out to the Dictator. If so, the sailors were to move northward along the beach and wave their caps as a signal.

If the shore party couldn't launch a lifeboat, the sailors were to move south. Then they were to attach a rope to the other end of the ship's boat so that it could be drawn back and forth between the ship and the shore.

When the boat was hauled back, Jorgensen intended to land his wife and son, who still remained below in the cabin.

Jorgensen watched anxiously as the boat made its way to shore. Two of the sailors alternately pulled and backed with the oars, a third used the steering oar to keep the boat pointed into the sea, while the fourth man bailed the water out.

As the boat reached the shore breakers it capsized and threw the men into the water. Surfmen watching every movement as the boat approached the shore were quick to haul the sailors onto the beach.

On board the bark, Captain Jorgensen kept his binoculars fixed on shore, waiting for his men to give him a signal. What he saw, however, was a crowd gathering about his sailors, now wrapped in blankets by their rescuers.

The signal he waited for was not to come. The men, overwhelmed by the excitement of being saved, failed to carry out their captain's instructions. Jorgensen was bitterly disappointed, for he planned to send his wife and son ashore in the next boat trip. The boat, though small, would save them all, he believed.

With the four seamen ashore, the Life Saving Station crews and the spectators ashore now knew that the stricken vessel was the Norwegian bark Dictator. The fact that the captain's wife and son were on board excited the onlookers, many of whom began asking why the lifesavers weren't launching their lifeboat.

Keeper Edward Drinkwater, in charge of the rescue operations, looked out toward the stricken vessel and pondered his next move. The wind-blown biting rain stung his face as his eyes measured the height and force of the pounding waves; his heart felt a deep compassion toward the luckless people on board the bark rolling helplessly in the surf. Should he send for the surfboat still back at the Seatack Life Saving Station? Would the surfboat flip over and capsize as did the ship's boat when it hit the shoreline? Could he risk the lives of his own life saving crew when he knew that their chances of reaching the beached ship were minimal in view of the stormy

Artist's drawing of a life car used by the United States Life Saving Service to rescue people from shipwrecks when weather prevented the launching of lifeboats. Photo courtesy of United States Coast Guard.

weather? There was a woman and a child aboard that ship; this alone demanded that he do his utmost to save them. Send the boat or try again with the breeches buoy? Or should he delay his decision, hoping for an improvement in the weather?

Drinkwater made his decision.

"We won't send the surfboat out. It's unsafe."

His ruling sent a shockwave through the two life saving crews and the crowd of onlookers.

"My God, man! There are living souls out there!" someone cried.

"You're supposed to go out! It's your duty!," shouted another familiar with the unwritten code of the Life Saving Service: "You have to go out, but you don't have to come back."

Drinkwater replied that it would be impossible for the surfboat crew to pull the oars against the high winds and raging sea. Some of the surfmen agreed with their leader's decision, knowing from experience how difficult it would be to launch a boat against the powerful onrushing sea.

Support came also from several of the local citizens familiar with the sea and Virginia Beach coastal waters. It would be insane recklessness, next to madness, to have tried to launch a boat in the breaking surf, they contended.

Among the dissenters was W. S. Price, a local fisherman who taunted Drinkwater and his life saving crews for not attempting to launch their surfboat.

Price, who owned two fishing boats and had a crew of twelve fishermen at his command, offered a sum of money to anybody who would bring one of his boats to the scene.

"Bring me a boat and I'll take her out myself to the wreck," he challenged.

There were no takers, nor did Price himself order any of his fishermen to fetch one of his boats.

Several bystanders, including one of the rescued Norwegian sailors, urged Drinkwater to let them go out in the Seatack Life Saving Station's surfboat, but he rejected their offer.

Belatedly, the Dictator sailors told Keeper Drinkwater of their captain's plan for the shore party to tie another line to their small boat so it could be hauled out to the ship and then be pulled back to shore with people from the bark

Drinkwater rejected this suggestion also. "The boat will be filled with water as soon as it leaves the beach. The current will swing it broadside to the sea and fill it with water at once. It is utterly impracticable to do what your captain suggests," said Drinkwater.

Someone urged that the life car—an enclosed iron boat with pointed ends and a watertight hatch—be sent out to the ship. It was hauled back and forth between a wrecked ship and the shore in the same manner as Captain Jorgensen had suggested be done with his small boat. The car, which could hold six to eight passengers, would tumble about and be submerged in the surf, but the persons inside would be dry. There were many instances in which the life car had been used successfully by the Life Saving Service when the weather prevented the launching of lifeboats.

In a furious storm on January 12, 1850, The British ship Ayrshire, with 202 passengers and crew aboard, ran aground in a blinding snowstorm four hundred yards off Squan Beach, New Jersey. While unable to send out a lifeboat, the crew of New Jersey Life Saving Station Number Four saved 201 of the 202 people on board by use of the life car.

Keeper Edward Drinkwater rejected another suggestion to use an available life saving device. The life car would remain at the Life Saving Station. The surf was too rough and the current too strong for the sailors to haul the heavy life car to their ship, he reasoned.

"It would take thirty persons to pull the life car through the surf," he said.

The tide was now getting lower, and Drinkwater decided to make another attempt to use the breeches buoy. He made a signal to the people aboard the Dictator to bend the end of the whip they had used to slacken their boat ashore to the buoy in place of the broken line. This was done, and on a signal from Captain Jorgensen the empty buoy was drawn to the shore to test it. The buoy worked perfectly. The sailors then hauled it back to the ship.

Captain Jorgensen turned to Seaman Jakob Mell and asked: "Are you ready to try it again?"

"Yes Sir!" said Mell, and climbed into the breeches buoy.

The buoy was hauled ashore slowly, and the rescuers strained every muscle in order to keep the sailor out of the cold water as much as possible.

Finally he reached shore safely. It was now nearly three in the afternoon, and the tide was at its lowest. The rescue of Mell encouraged Captain Jorgensen. He would now prepare to send his wife Johanne ashore in the buoy.

Directing the carpenter to be the next man to get into the buoy, Jorgensen said: "If, after you get ashore, you think it is possible for Mrs. Jorgensen to make the passage, walk south and wave your hat; and, if you think it is unsafe, go the other way."

As the carpenter was being hauled ashore, Johanne and her son Carl were brought up from the cabin and stood sheltered in the small deckhouse on the poop. Watching the carpenter being dipped into the sea and then jerked skyward as the bark rolled, tautening and then slackening the buoy line, Johanne Jorgensen lamented that "I would rather die on board than suffer that terrible ordeal."

Her husband tried to calm her, but clutching her son, she cried, "Oh, Jorgen, I'm afraid."

Once safely ashore, the half dazed and frightened carpenter failed to carry out Jorgensen's instructions, nor did he tell anyone in the rescue party of the captain's intention to send his wife ashore in the buoy.

For some reason, the shore party delayed sending the buoy off again. When it did go, keeper Drinkwater, who thought the lines were again fouled out at the wreck, sent a written message in a bottle: "Keep the whip clear and we will bring you ashore."

Captain Jorgensen, puzzled over the delay and the message, found the lines at the ship to be clear since the first man was landed safely.

Shortly after the carpenter was rescued, the Dictator crewmen discovered that the sternpost had been wrung out of place. The seas were beginning to wash into the hull.

A sailor yelled, "We're breaking up!"

Realizing that his ship was doomed, Captain Jorgensen went to his wife at the deckhouse.

"Paua, we're breaking up; you must get into the buoy."

Her eyes reflected terror. "I'm scared. I can't do it."

"There's no need to be afraid. The buoy is working. They are going to save us," Jorgensen reassured her.

As they emerged from the deckhouse, a huge wave dashed over the deck and came near sweeping everyone into the sea. While Jorgensen clutched desperately to his son Carl, who cried for his mother, a seaman grabbed his wife as she slid across the deck toward the railing.

The Dictator's timbers groaned and cracked with every heave of the sea, and the foaming waters kept washing over the deck

Facing imminent disaster, Jorgensen maintained an outward calm as he convinced his wife that she had to climb up the rigging and get into the breeches buoy.

"But my boy, my poor boy!" she cried.

"He will come next. Mister Nilsen will bring him ashore."

Jorgensen handed his son Carl to First Mate Cornelius Nilsen, then sent Second Mate Julius Andersen and another sailor aloft into the crosstrees to see that the breeches buoy was clear.

With great difficulty Jorgensen helped his wife up to the buoy, only to learn that the slings of the buoy were jammed against the rigging by the hauling line. The sailors tried to free the buoy sufficiently to enable Mrs. Jorgensen to get into it, but they couldn't budge it.

The mast swayed from side to side as if it had become unstepped at the keelson.

Johanne became hysterical, crying, "No! No! I can't do it!," as her husband held her in the rigging, waiting for the sailors trying frantically to free the buoy.

His strength ebbing and the men unable to prepare the buoy, Jorgensen descended to the deck with his wife.

At this point, one of the youngest members of the crew, a slightly-built boy, ran up the rigging and squeezed himself between the slings down into the buoy.

The surprised captain signaled the beach for the buoy to be hauled ashore. By letting the buoy be drawn ashore, he thought he would be given another opportunity for his wife to use it.

The heavy seas rushing over the deck caused the rail around the quarterdeck to crumble, freeing the spanker vangs and allowing the gaff to swing from side to side with each roll of the ship. The situation aboard ship was becoming critical, but the captain and the two mates went aloft and secured the gaff.

By this time it was late in the afternoon, and while the gaff was being secured, another sailor had been rescued by the buoy.

The Dictator was now rapidly breaking to pieces. The stern was gone, and the poop deck, upon which the remainder of the crew was standing, slanted down into the water.

With a shattering crack, the bark broke in two admidships, so that the forward part of the hull was nearly submerged.

The breeches buoy had returned from the shore and was hanging at the mizzen crosstrees, but as darkness set in, and the deck frame crunched apart beneath their feet, those on board failed to notice the breeches buoy awaiting their deliverance.

Death was coming to the Dictator. Those still on board knew that the end was near. Each also knew that he would have only himself to depend upon in the final crash. They began looking about for what might be the safest place to be when the end came.

Captain Jorgensen lashed his wife to the standard of the windmill pump at the forward part of the poop, and held the child in his arm. The two mates, Cornelius Nilsen and Julius Andersen, together with a seaman, Andreas Isaacsen, climbed forward to the jib boom, but Jorgensen preferred to remain where he was, hoping that the deck would soon become detached and float off and carry him and his family safely to the beach.

The ship's steward, a black man named Saint Clair, climbed into the mizzen crosstrees.

Two other crew members, Ole Olsen and a French sailor named Jean Baptiste, decided to take their chances with the captain. Olsen, however, became unnerved and sprang from the ship in a desperate attempt to swim ashore. Olsen was known to be a good swimmer, but he was too heavily clothed, and soon disappeared in the surf.

It was now dark, and the rain prevented anyone from distinguishing signals from the shore, nor could any signals be made by those on ship. All hope of outside help had been abandoned by those left on the Dictator.

Jorgensen decided to make one last attempt to save his wife and child. He had saved the ship's ladder for this moment. He told Johanne how, together, they would try to float to shore on the ladder.

Resigned to her fate, Johanne answered: "Don't you think it better that we die here together?"

To this he answered, in a reassuring voice, that the ladder was their only resource left for survival, and that it was large and strong enough to carry them safely to the shore.

There were only two ring-shaped life preservers on board the bark Jorgensen placed one on his wife and tied it securely to her body. Then he put the other life preserver on himself, lashing his son Carl to his breast. Now he was ready to descend to the ladder.

Jorgensen embraced his wife and told her that Seaman Baptiste would lower her to the ladder.

"Good-bye, Paua," he said, choked with emotion. "Keep your mouth shut. We will get ashore all right."

Jorgensen and Baptiste then placed the ladder overboard, and the captain lowered himself into the foaming water.

On reaching the water, Jorgensen missed the ladder, but landed between it and the ship's side. The heavy seas made the ladder an elusive target. Each time he tried to get on it, the ladder would capsize. Carl screamed with fright as his father fought to climb on to the ladder, while all the time trying to keep his son's head out of water.

Suddenly a big wave threw Jorgensen away from the ladder, and when he rose to the surface he saw his horror-stricken wife at the rail, her hands clasped as in prayer.

The strong current swept the powerless captain towards and around the after part of the wreck, where the surf was the heaviest. A huge wave carried the father and son into the cavity of the hull where the stern had broken off. The water around them teemed with the heaving and grinding mass of floating timbers of the cargo. Miraculously they escaped death as the next surge of water swept them out of the hull and into the open sea.

Little Carl, who had swallowed much water, moaned pitifully as his father tried to shield him from the dangerous wreckage floating around them.

Jorgensen had made his way about half to the shore when a wave surged over him and drove him to the bottom. When he struggled to the surface he discovered to his horror that the child had been torn away from his body. The frenzied captain, fighting the surf, swam about searching for his son, shouting, "Carl! Carl!"

Realizing that his son was lost, Jorgen Jorgensen caught and clung to a piece of wreckage that floated near him. Soon he found himself on a sandbank. With his remaining strength, Jorgensen crawled up on the beach, a few hundred yards to the north of the Dictator wreckage.

Lying on the beach, the almost unconscious captain collected his senses and stumbled toward an open fire he had spotted on the beach. Some of the surfmen around the fire saw him approaching in the dark and ran to his aid. Jorgensen was taken to the Seatack Life Saving Station, where he was greeted by the survivors of his crew who were keeping warm around the messroom stove.

When the captain was swept away from the Dictator, the faithful Jean Baptiste remained with Mrs. Jorgensen until the end. Known to be a powerful swimmer, the Frenchman could well have attempted to swim clear of the wreckage and save himself. Soon after Jorgensen was lost to sight from the ship, a wave dashed over the deck and swept Johanne Jorgensen and the gallant Jean Baptiste overboard. Their struggle was immense, but they both drowned.

Shortly after Mrs. Jorgensen and Baptiste were washed overboard, the entire after and midship portion of the Dictator went completely to pieces. The cracking and breaking of the timbers could be heard on shore over the howling of the storm.

The mizzenmast fell and carried Steward Saint Clair to his watery grave. The mizzenmast also carried with it the breeches buoy equipment, dashing the last hope of rescuing anyone still aboard the Dictator.

The young sailor Isaacsen who, together with the two mates, had sought refuge on the jib boom, was washed overboard and drowned in the raging surf.

First Mate Nilsen and Second Mate Andersen were now the last two men left on the Dictator. Andersen suggested that the two take their chances together in an effort to swim ashore. Nilsen, who had lashed himself to the boom, refused to leave because he couldn't swim.

As Andersen was trying to convince Nilsen to try to save himself, a heavy sea crashed over them and Andersen was thrown floundering into the surf. He struggled desperately in the turbulent surf, and several times was nearly crushed by the floating wreckage. Nearing the shore he cried out for help and several surfmen waded out into the surf and pulled him safely ashore.

The first mate drowned when the forward part of the bark was demolished about eight o'clock in the evening.

The wreck was total. The broken timbers of the hull and the cargo of pine timber were scattered along the beach. The Dictator, once a proud and gallant sailing ship, was no more. The sea, which can be both kind and cruel, calm and angry, had chosen to destroy the aging Norwegian bark and those who sailed her.

None are more familiar with the hazards of seafaring than the people of the little towns along the Norwegian coasts. When a man is lost at sea the people of the far north make a laconic comment. "'Han ble,'" they say. "He stayed."

Those who stayed in the Dictator tragedy were Mrs. Johanne Pauline Jorgensen and her son Carl Zealand, First Mate Cornelius Nilsen, Seamen Ole Olsen, Jean Baptiste, Andreas Isaacsen, and Steward Saint Clair.

Survivors were Captain Jorgen Martinius Jorgensen, Second Mate Julius Andersen, Seamen John Syverken, Karl Olsen, Anton Berg, Jakob Mell, John Pettersen, Christian Nilsen, Axel Johansen, and Charles Josef.

Lion-headed stern piece from the Dictator. Photo by William O. Foss

CHAPTER FOUR

REST IN PEACE

It was over.

The sea had won.

Slowly the surfmen began gathering their rescue gear, and the curious and shocked onlookers from the Princess Anne Hotel returned to their warm and comfortable rooms.

While the Cape Henry Life Saving Station crew returned to their station, Captain Edward Drinkwater ordered some of his men to patrol the beach until midnight in search of possible survivors or bodies. He returned to the Seatack Life Saving Station about 8:30 that evening with the Dictator's Second Mate Andersen, the last person to be rescued.

The survivors of the Norwegian bark were supplied with warm clothing made available by the Women's National Relief Association. This charitable organization, established in 1880, provided each life saving station in the United States with a box of clothing and personal hygiene supplies for shipwreck survivors. The association also furnished the stations with extra sleeping cots, blankets, and medical supplies.

By sunrise the next morning, Saturday, March 28, the weather had improved. It had stopped raining, but the surf continued to be rough. Wreckage and cargo from the Dictator were strewn along the beach in front of the Seatack Life Saving Station and the Princess Anne Hotel.

Captain Jorgensen walked up and down the beach for miles searching for his wife and son. He knew he would never see them alive again, but he wanted to find them. The sea had taken his loved ones, leaving him with only memories.

The weary captain stood silent, his tear-filled eyes glaring hopelessly into the sea. Tired and dazed, he was unaware of the foaming sea water washing about his feet.

Survivors of the Dictator in front of the Seatack Life Saving Station. Captain Jorgen M. Jorgensen is the fifth man from the right. Photo courtesy of Miss Cornelia R. Holland, Virginia Beach, Virginia.

Captain Jorgensen and his crew members remained at the Seatack Life Saving Station until Easter Sunday, March 29, when they left for Norfolk under arrangements made by the Norwegian consul at Norfolk, Colonel William Lamb and his associate, Hugh Amal.

Before the Norwegian sailors embarked on the train for Norfolk, they were met by a group of hotel guests and excursionists who had come out from Norfolk to view the remains of the shipwreck. Crittenden, manager of the Princess Anne Hotel, made a short speech and then presented the sailors with four hundred dollars that had been collected for them by the hotel guests. Captain Jorgensen was given one hundred dollars, the widow of First Mate Nilsen was to receive fifty-five dollars, Second Mate Andersen received forty dollars, and the remainder was split among the other eight survivors.

During their Norfolk stay, Captain Jorgensen was the guest of Hugo Amal at his Huntersville home, while the crew was quartered at the Furlong Boarding House on Plume Street

On Saturday, March 28, patrols from the Cape Henry Life Saving Station found the first two bodies of Dictator seamen. The bodies were turned over to Harry D. Oliver, funeral director on Church Street in Norfolk, on order of the Norwegian consul.

The body of Johanne Pauline Jorgensen was found on the evening of Easter Sunday, March 29, on the beach in the vicinity of the Princess Anne Hotel. The remains of Jean Baptiste, the French sailor who had stayed with her until the end, were also found near the hotel. All bodies, except for those of the captain's son and the ship's steward, had now been found.

Funerals for Mrs. Jorgensen, Jean Baptiste, and the Norwegian sailors were held on March 31 at the Elmswood Cemetery in Norfolk.

Ships in Hampton Roads, including several Norwegian ships, flew their national flags at half staff in tribute to the shipwreck victims.

The sailors were buried in the morning in the lot of the Seamen's Friend Society, while Mrs. Jorgensen's body was interred in the private lot of Joseph Klepper, owner of the Rhine Wine Rooms, a restaurant opposite the Opera House on Church Street

Prior to the funeral, Norwegian Lutheran memorial services were held for Mrs. Jorgensen at the Oliver funeral home. The memorial services were attended by Captain Jorgensen, the surviving Dictator crew, and sailors from other Norwegian ships in Hampton Roads. Captain Flood, underwriting agent for Lloyd's in New York, conducted the memorial services. He was assisted by Captain Nilson of the yacht Lourine, Captain Nicholson of the Norwegian steamship Dana, and Hugo Amal, representing the Norwegian consulate's office.

Funeral services for Mrs. Jorgensen were held at the Granby Street Methodist Episcopal Church and were conducted by the Reverend J. B. Merritt, chaplain of the Seamen's Friend Society, assisted by the Reverend W. E. Evans, pastor of the Granby Street Church.

News of the tragic shipwreck, and especially of Captain Jorgensen's personal loss of wife and child, stirred the heartstrings of the community. Many people attended the funeral services, and a profusion of beautiful flowers and wreaths were sent by sympathizers.

The body of the Dictator's steward Saint Clair was found April 3 near the Seatack Life Saving Station and was buried at Virginia Beach.

The next day, Saturday, April 4, the body of Captain Jorgensen's son, Carl Zealand, was found in the breakers near the Princess Anne Hotel by Surfman James Burlas walking his early morning patrol.

Keeper Drinkwater immediately notified the Norwegian consul in hopes of getting in touch with Captain Jorgensen, but the Norwegian master had departed Norfolk a day earlier for New York, where he boarded a ship sailing for Norway.

Before leaving Norfolk, Jorgensen visited his wife's grave at the Elmwood Cemetery. Kneeling before the flower-covered grave, Jorgensen offered a prayer and said his last good-bye to his beloved "Paua." Tenderly he picked a collection of flowers that he would take home to Norway. He would preserve them; they would be his link with "Paua."

Carl Zealand's body was brought to Norfolk by undertaker Oliver, and the child was buried Saturday evening with his mother; Chaplain Merritt conducted the services.

The Dictator's figurehead standing at Sixteenth Street and the oceanfront in Virginia Beach. Photo taken in the 1930s, courtesy of Virginia Beach Public Libraries.

Some time after the funeral, a group of Norfolk citizens had a memorial stone placed at the head of the grave of Mrs. Jorgensen and her son.

The inscription on front of the stone, now hardly visible after years of erosion, states:

JOHANNE PAULINE

and

CARL ZEALAND

Beloved Wife and Child of

J. M. JORGENSEN

Born in Kragero, Norway

Shipwrecked at Virginia Beach

March 27, 1891

On the reverse side of the headstone one finds the same information written in Norwegian, with these added words:

Lenge Leve Din Minde

Hvil I Fred

Translation: Long Live Your Memory

Rest In Peace

Some of the Dictator sailors followed their captain to New York, where they found sailing ship masters eager to hire experienced hands. Others found employment on ships in the Hampton Roads. One sailor, Anton Berg, decided to try his luck ashore, and was hired as a rigger at the Norfolk Naval Shipyard in Portsmouth.

While the Dictator was a total loss, the Norwegian bark had been insured for fifteen thousand dollars. Her cargo of pine timber, valued at 9,825 dollars, was salvaged. Most of her timber was later sold and used for the interior woodwork of the Saint Luke's Episcopal Church, then under construction on Granby Street in Norfolk

As often happens in time of disaster, scavengers and souvenir hunters flocked to Virginia Beach in hopes of finding a curio or something of value from the ill-fated Norwegian sailing ship. Bernard Holland, for example, found the Dictator's stern piece, on which was

Grave marker for Mrs. Johanne Pauline Jorgensen and her son, Carl Zealand, in Elmwood Cemetery, Norfolk, Virginia. Photo by William O. Foss.

carved a lion's head, and a life preserver embossed with the name of the ship and its homeport, Moss.

The day after the shipwreck, Crittenden, manager of the Princess Anne Hotel, took his guest Emily Gregory for a ride along the beach in a buckboard. Looking into the rough surf, Emily spotted a large object. It proved to be the figurehead of the Dictator, a woman of heroic proportions draped in classic garments.

Crittenden had the figurehead retrieved and placed in the sands by the hotel, at what is now Sixteenth Street and the oceanfront, with the figurehead facing the sea, a memorial to those who perished.

That figurehead, which the sea had ripped from the prow of the bark Dictator, was to play an important role in the future of Virginia Beach.

CHAPTER FIVE

THE INVESTIGATION

Edward Drinkwater, Keeper of the Seatack Life Saving Station, was severely criticized for his handling of the Dictator rescue operation.

He was also highly praised for doing his very best under extremely adverse conditions.

Most of the criticism came from guests at the Princess Anne Hotel, although there were some complaints about Drinkwater's actions from local citizens. The hotel guests, most of them accustomed to living a life of comfort and unappreciative of the dangers faced daily by those who make their living by the sea or, as in the case of the lifesavers, risking their lives in fighting the sea, were excited and distraught over the tragedy.

The fact that Captain Drinkwater had not attempted to use either his station's lifeboat or life car in the rescue effort drew the greatest criticism. The bad weather conditions, especially the strong wind and rough surf, were Drinkwater's reasons for not ordering his men to haul the lifeboat or life car to the rescue scene. He believed that it would have been useless to try to launch these lifesaving apparatus in the treacherous weather conditions. Lives could have been needlessly lost, he contended.

Those who supported Keeper Drinkwater were, for the most part, experienced watermen and fishermen, many of whom remembered that the weather conditions during the Dictator rescue attempt were similar to those that prevailed on January 9, 1887, when five men of the Life Saving Service lost their lives trying to rescue the crew of the German ship Elisabeth, grounded in a blinding snow storm near the Little Island Life Saving Station.

Unable to fire a line aboard the stricken ship, Abel Belanga, keeper of the Little Island Life Saving Station, picked a lifesaving boat crew comprised of surfmen from his own station and from the Dam Neck Mills Life Saving Station, whose men assisted in the rescue operation.

As they approached the ship, aground on the outer edge of the bar, the lifesavers discovered that the German crew had abandoned ship and had sought refuge in their own lifeboat, attached to the stricken ship with a rope.

Keeper Belanga got some of the Germans into his surfboat, and as he turned his craft shoreward, an immense wave swept over the two boats, capsizing both boats and throwing every man into the sea.

Keeper Belanga and four surfmen, including his brother James E. and brother-in-law Joseph Spratley, and the entire German crew of twenty-two died in the disaster. Only two surfmen survived.

J. W. Etheridge, superintendent of the Sixth District of the United States Life Saving Service, went to the Seatack Life Saving Station to discuss the rescue efforts with Drinkwater.

It turned out to be a bitter meeting: Drinkwater claimed vehemently that he had done his best with the equipment he had; Etheridge charged that the keeper had failed to properly utilize all the rescue equipment at his disposal.

"You made a mistake," said Etheridge in an ominous tone as he left the station.

On Sunday morning, March 29, 1891, First Lieutenant Thomas D. Walker of the United States Revenue Marine and Assistant Inspector of the Life Saving Stations, arrived in Norfolk by train from Washington, D.C. Proceeding to Virginia Beach, he arrived at the Seatack Life Saving Station about one o'clock in the afternoon and began an investigation into the Dictator rescue operations.

Under strict rules issued by Sumner Increase Kimball, chief of the United States Treasury Department's Revenue Marine Division, and General Superintendent of the United States Life Saving Service, a thorough investigation was conducted whenever a shipwreck resulted in the loss of life. An Assistant Inspector, subordinate to the General Inspector, would investigate all the circumstances connected with the disaster to ascertain whether any officers or employees of the Life Saving Service could be accused of neglect, errors of judgment, or misconduct in the rescue operations. Dereliction of duty of any sort was to be rewarded with instant dismissal.

Lieutenant Walker began his investigation, conducted at the Seatack Life Saving Station, by first interviewing Captain Jorgen M. Jorgensen and Keeper Edward Drinkwater. Each gave his own version of the disaster, and the two principals differed on how the rescue could have been effected in several instances.

Jörgensen denied that his crew did not know how to work the breeches buoy and complained that the buoy was kept too long on shore before being returned to the ship between rescue trips.

Jorgensen was bitter that he had not been permitted to haul the small boat back to the ship once the four sailors had landed. He had wanted the shore party to attach a line to the other end of the Dictator's boat so it could have been drawn back and forth between the vessel and the beach. Jorgensen wanted to send his wife and son ashore in the next boat trip, which never came about.

Drinkwater countered that it would have been unsafe to use the bark's boat against the heavy surf.

"The conditions of a storm appear very different to the crew of a stranded vessel than they do to a life saving crew," Drinkwater explained. "The ship's crew are back of the surf and cannot see it, while the life savers on the beach are in front of it and can see the danger."

Captain Jorgensen, a strong man who, with a cool and collected composure, had spent all his energies to saving his crew and beloved ones, was in tears, his frame quivering with anguish, as he related to Lieutenant Walker his final efforts to save his wife and child.

Lieutenant Walker obtained a variety of professional and nonprofessional testimony from members of the life saving crews, the surviving crewmembers of the Dictator, fishermen and boatsmen who helped in the rescue effort, and from the Easter holiday guests at the Princess Anne Hotel.

After having had breakfast at the Seatack Life Saving Station on March 31, Lieutenant Walker ended his investigation into the Dictator shipwreck, and returned to Washington to write his report and findings.

The Tidewater community, speculating about the results, was in quite a stir over the investigation. Some members of the seafaring community, strong-minded individuals who seldom take kindly to authority, looked upon the one-man investigation with skepticism.

One of the leading local newspapers, The Norfolk Landmark, in an editorial appearing on the day of Lieutenant Walker's departure, lamented that Captain Drinkwater had not taken the life car to the beach, but suggested that "Drinkwater may be able to explain all these things." The editorial then declared that "We shall believe he did his utmost until the contrary fully appears."

Twenty-one year old Herman Drinkwater, Captain Edward Drinkwater's second oldest son, a surfman at the False Cape Life Saving Station, offered this thought on the investigation: "My father will be vindicated if the opinions of the life savers and wreckers are considered, but if the outsiders are listened to then the opposite result might be reached." A wrecker is a person employed in recovering wrecked or disabled vessels or their cargoes, as in the interest of the owners or underwriters.

Edward Drinkwater had spent most of his life earning a living from the sea, either as a fisherman or as a member of the United States Life Saving Service.

He was born on April 13, 1844, in Yarmouth, Maine, of parents who had emigrated from Glasgow, Scotland. The family moved to North Carolina, first settling in Stumpy Point, later moving to Roanoke Island, where Edward began to earn his living by fishing in the Roanoke, Albemarle, and Pamlico Sounds.

After General Robert E. Lee surrendered to General Ulysses S. Grant at Appomattox Court House on April 9, 1865, and thus ended the Civil War, there were many young Southern men who wondered how they were going to make a living in a war-torn and defeated South. While Edward Drinkwater had not fought in the war, he saw its end as an opportunity to strike out for new adventures. Impressed with the way the United States Navy had bottled up Southern forces and made the Confederate Navy an ineffective force, Drinkwater offered his services to the United States Navy. He reasoned that the Navy could well make use of his navigational expertise and experience as a fisherman.

On May 17, 1865, Drinkwater accepted an appointment as acting ensign in the Navy, and reported to his first duty as a pilot aboard the tug U.S.S. Clinton, then at the Norfolk Navy Yard.

Drinkwater's naval career was short-lived, however, as the Navy decided to discharge many of its officers when it became evident that they were not needed in the post-war years.

One month after Drinkwater entered the service, on June 17, the Navy Department's Bureau of Navigation issued honorable discharge orders to a number of ensigns, including Drinkwater, who was then in Philadelphia aboard the tug U.S.S. Martin. He was given one month's leave of absence, at end of which, on July 19, he was officially separated from the Navy while at his home on Roanoke Island.

Edward Drinkwater returned to his fishing and married Josephine Etheridge of Roanoke Island. Their first son, Horatio, was born in 1867. Edward and Josephine were to have fourteen children, thirteen boys and one girl.

A compassionate man, Drinkwater could be counted on to help people in need. As a fisherman, plying his trade in the storm-prone Carolina waters, Drinkwater often went to the aid of fellow fishermen endangered by foul weather and storms. His concern for fishermen and mariners who suffered the wrath of the infamous Carolina storms eventually led him to offer his services to the United States Life Saving Service.

On December 4, 1874, Drinkwater became keeper of the Life Saving Station at Oregon Inlet. His superiors noted that he was well qualified for the job, being a fisherman by trade and in sound physical condition. Drinkwater's superiors wrote that he was an "intelligent" man, and that his ability to perform the Life Saving Service duties were rated as "excellent."

Drinkwater remained in charge of the Oregon Inlet Station until March 6, 1879, when he became keeper of the Seatack Life Saving Station in Virginia Beach.

He left the Seatack station on January 28, 1886, to manage a hunt club established in Virginia Beach by a group of Norfolk businessmen. The club became known as the Drinkwater Club, but a few years later the businessmen built a new club at Twenty-Fourth Street and changed the name to the Atlantic Club.

Drinkwater also owned a team of horses, which he used to transport sportsmen to hunting areas in Virginia Beach and Princess Anne County.

These leisure time activities apparently did not interest Drinkwater too much, because on February 21, 1888, he replaced Joseph King as keeper of the Seatack Life Saving Station.

As an employee of the United States Life Saving Service, Edward Drinkwater had built an impeccable reputation; his superiors had on several occasions commended him for his excellent work, and his leadership was well recognized by those in the marine community.

During Drinkwater's tenure at the Seatack Life Saving Station, he and his surfmen performed many successful rescues. Unfortunately, few were known to the public. Shipwrecks in which all hands were saved seldom made the news; only disasters involving loss of life became widely publicized. Non-fatal shipwrecks were treated as routine, yet surfmen risked their lives in every rescue effort.

A violent hurricane struck the Virginia Beach and North Carolina coastlines on April 7, 1889, and surfmen in the Sixth District of the Life Saving Service were kept busy rescuing sailors from more than two dozen ships which were wrecked between Cape Henry and Cape Hatteras.

When the north patrol set out from the Seatack Station at midnight, April 7, the wind was blowing at hurricane rate from the north-northeast, at times exceeding one hundred miles an hour, as registered at the Signal Service Station at Cape Henry. The tide was high over all the beaches in the vicinity.

Shortly after midnight the patrol discovered the four-masted schooner Benjamin F. Poole of Providence, Rhode Island, ashore about a quarter of a mile north of the station. Drinkwater led his rescue party to the scene. The vessel had fortunately stranded only seventy-five yards from the shore, so there was no difficulty in throwing the shot line on board with the Lyle gun. Eight men were brought ashore by breeches buoy in as many trips.

When the master, Captain Hjalmar Charlton, learned that his ship, bound for Baltimore with coal, was not in immediate danger of breaking up, he and his first mate returned to the ship.

The Benjamin F. Poole was left so high and dry after the storm had passed that people could walk around her in low tide. The Merritt Wrecking Company took charge, and several attempts were made to float the ship, but to no avail.

Realizing that only a very abnormal high tide could float the vessel, the wreckers built a coffer dam around the ship, forming a dry dock of sorts. A heavy rope was put to the sea side with an anchor and marked by a buoy.

While waiting for the right storm to come, the captain married in July 1890, and he and his bride, Matilda Lowhermueller of Baltimore, spent their honeymoon aboard the stranded ship.

Not before September 28, 1890, after a three-day storm had struck Virginia Beach and raised the tide to a high level, was the wrecking company able to pull the Benjamin F. Poole off the beach.

When the April 7 midnight south patrol from the Cape Henry Life Saving Station failed to meet the north patrol from Seatack, he continued on, as directed by the Life Saving Service regulations, in order to learn the cause of the other's absence.

About a mile from the Seatack station he discovered a vessel stranded near the beach. He lit two Coston signals to inform those on board that help was coming.

Arriving at the scene where the Seatack crew were completing rescue of the crew of the Benjamin F. Poole, the Cape Henry surfman helped his comrades finish the job. Then the Seatack crew got some extra rescue gear and headed into the wind and rain for the second stricken ship.

The ship, the schooner Emma F. Hart of Camden, Maine, was rolling in the surf about a hundred yards from the shore. Drinkwater's crew trained the Lyle gun and threw the shot line on board at the first attempt. The crew of seven men with their baggage were landed without mishap by means of the breeches buoy, the last man reaching the shore about sunrise.

The Emma F. Hart was enroute from Bahama Islands to Boston with a freight of lumber. Her cargo was saved, but the vessel became a total loss.

When Drinkwater and his men returned to their station around nine o'clock in the morning, they were quite tired from their two rescue efforts and their fight with the elements. They had no sooner settled down when a messenger from the Princess Anne Hotel arrived to tell them of a ship in distress near the hotel.

The surfmen quickly gathered their gear and hurried toward the endangered ship. Since the tide was running high, the surfmen had to haul their apparatus along the narrow gauge railroad track which ran some distance parallel to the shore, then work their way with considerable difficulty over the sand hills and through the hollows back of the beach until they reached the Rudee Inlet

When they arrived at Rudee Inlet, they found that the schooner Northampton, an "oyster pungy" from Cherrystone, Virginia, had come ashore and was being broken to pieces. A fisherman told them that the vessel had struck a little more than half an hour before their arrival. The lone survivor, John Moody, was being cared for at a nearby farmhouse.

There was nothing more that the tired life saving crew could do. Three crewmembers of the oyster boat drowned in the disaster; they were beyond the reach of human aid.

A trite saying goes: "You win some and you lose some."

On April 7, 1889, Keeper Edward Drinkwater and his surfmen of the Seatack Life Saving Station won some and lost some.

———————

On April 6, 1891, First Lieutenant Thomas D. Walker of the United States Revenue Marine submitted the report on his investigation into the wreck of the Norwegian bark Dictator near the Seatack Life Saving

Station to Sumner Increase Kimball, General Superintendent of the United States Life Saving Service.

Describing the Dictator shipwreck and reviewing the failure of the station crews to rescue all the people of the bark, Walker said:

"There can be no question as to the state of the weather. It was bad. The storm was one of exceptional severity. The great distance of the vessel from the shore was also an important factor. When the bark first grounded it was impossible to reach her from the shore with even the smallest line used by the service. Account should also be taken of the great violence of the sea, which was breaking into surf in places a considerable distance outside the spot where she fetched up. It would seem, therefore, that the odds were against the successful manipulation of the breeches buoy apparatus. The latter was on the ground in good season, but as shown by this report the greatest difficulty was encountered in getting it rigged, and it was largely due to the efforts of the crew of the bark, under the intelligent direction of Captain Jorgensen, that it was rigged at all. When this was accomplished additional obstacles hindered the beachmen, the rolling of the vessel, under the pressure of the enormous seas against her broadside, and the swift current along the shore making the handling of the apparatus difficult as well as exceedingly dangerous to those whom it was intended to relieve, and much precious time was lost. It is contended by some that the boat could have been used to advantage at low water, which was between two and three o'clock in the afternoon. Keeper Drinkwater, who was in charge of the operations, declares very positively that at no time during the day could a boat have been launched."

Lieutenant Walker's report continued: "In my opinion, the only possible time when there was a chance for pulling the boat out was at low water, and even then there was no certainty of success. Except at that time, with the wind blowing with a velocity of thirty or forty miles an hour, I believe it would have been found a physical impossibility to propel a boat by oars against the wind and sea. Nevertheless it is to be regretted that the boat was not upon the ground and an attempt made. There was too much at stake to rely upon any one means of rescue.

"In conclusion, if neither the breeches buoy nor the surfboat could be effectively used, the question recurs, had Drinkwater exhausted the means placed at his disposal by the Government for the salvation of the helpless people on the wreck? The answer is No! He had the life car. The buoy was working badly, and if in his judgment the boat could not be used, why did he not send to the station for the car? There were scores of people from the Virginia Beach Hotel and from the adjacent country ready and willing to do his bidding, and the life car could have been hurried to the scene in short order if he had but given the word. It became known when Captain Jorgensen sent his boat ashore that there was a woman and a child on board; it must also have been known that difficulty would be encountered, from the way the gear fouled, in rescuing them. If therefore, when the captain sent his message for the boat, Drinkwater's experience taught him that the boat service was impracticable, why did he not grasp the full needs of the situation and send for what he must have known would be a safe and almost certain means of rescue, the life car? If there ever was an occasion which seemed to require the use of the car this was one. It could have been drawn to and from the ship by a single line in the manner proposed by Captain Jorgensen for his frail open boat; there was no danger of its swamping, and under the circumstances it was by all odds the safest method that could have been resorted to for the rescue of the people on the wreck. In this lamentable case it is clear from his failure to bring into operation all the resources of the station that Drinkwater was not equal to the emergency. He probably did the best he could with the gear he took with him, but his neglect to send for other appliances when there seemed to be need of them was certainly an inexcusable error of judgment.

"Apply the conditions that surrounded the Dictator to a large ocean steamer crowded with passengers and what would have been the result?

"In view of all these things I submit the conclusion that the removal of Keeper Edward Drinkwater would be for the best interests of the Life Saving Service."

Lieutenant Walker's report accurately described the events of the Dictator tragedy and the efforts of the Seatack and Cape Henry surfmen's rescue efforts, but to whom did he listen when he drew his conclusions in the case?

Recall the words of Herman Drinkwater, the keeper's son, on the possible outcome of the investigation: "My father will be vindicated if the opinions of the life savers and wreckers are considered, but if the outsiders are listened to then the opposite result might be reached."

On April 4, two days before Lieutenant Walker submitted his report, the New York Evening Post published a letter to the editor in which its author, who called himself Humanitas, wrote a scathing denunciation of the Life Service's handling of the Dictator rescue effort.

Extract.

Treasury Department.
Office of the General Superintendent
Life-Saving Service,
Washington, D. C., *April 6* 189*1*.

J. I. Kimball, Esq.,
General Superintendent,
U. S. Life-Saving Service.

Sir:

In obedience to your order of the 28th ultimo, directing an investigation of the circumstances attending the wreck of the Norwegian bark Dictator, near the Seatack Station (Sixth District) on the 27th ultimo, I have the honor to submit the following report

x   x   x   x   x   x   x   x

I therefore feel constrained to report that in my judgment Keeper Drinkwater was not equal to the emergency and that he failed to utilize all the resources of his station. It is probable that he did the best he could with the appliances he used, but his failure to exhaust every means within reach betrays inexcusable error of judgment.

Apply the conditions that surrounded the Dictator to a large ocean steamer crowded with passengers and what would have been the result?

In view of all these things I submit the conclusion that the removal of Keeper Edward Drinkwater would be for the best interests of the Life-Saving Service.

Respectfully yours,
Thomas D. Walker,
1st Lieutenant U. S. R. M.,
Asst. Inspector Life-Saving Stations.

Extract from the recommendation by Thomas D. Walker that "removal of Edward Drinkwater would be for the best interests of the Live Saving Service." From the files of the United States Life Saving Service, National Archives and Records Service.

Explaining that he was one of the guests at the Princess Anne Hotel at the time of the shipwreck, Humanitas complained bitterly about every phase of the rescue operations, challenging the Government to prevent a recurrence of such a tragedy.

One sentence in Humanitas' letter requires special attention. It reads: "What if this vessel had been a New Orleans or Savannah steamer with perhaps a hundred souls on board?"

In his report to Superintendent Kimball, Lieutenant Walker had expressed the same thought when he wrote: "Apply the conditions that surrounded the Dictator to a large ocean steamer crowded with passengers and what would have been the result?"

This leads to another question.

Whose testimony influenced Lieutenant Walker to recommend the dismissal of Keeper Edward Drinkwater?

On April 20, Superintendent Kimball ordered that Edward Drinkwater be notified that his resignation, to take effect upon the appointment and qualification of his successor, would be accepted if tendered at once.

———

A broken-hearted Drinkwater, his life as a faithful public servant shattered by a single event, sat alone in his small office on the second floor of the Seatack Life Saving Station. He looked at the daily log book, noted the remarks of the patrols, and stared for several minutes at a blank sheet of paper.

Then he wrote:

Virginia Beach. May 4, 1891
To the Secretary of the Treasury, USA, in care of Superintendent Six Life Saving District.
Sir. I hereby tender my resignation as Keeper of Seatack Life Saving Station.

> Respectfully yours
> Edward Drinkwater
> Keeper

There were many people in the Tidewater area who were not satisfied with the investigation of Drinkwater and his subsequent forced resignation. When he departed the Life Saving Service, The Norfolk Landmark of May 31 carried a lengthy editorial in which it discussed the circumstances around his resignation. Reflecting the doubt of many concerning the fairness of the action of the Life Saving Service against Drinkwater, the editorial commented: "If the fault was

Edward Drinkwater's letter of resignation, from the files of the United States Life Saving Service, National Archives and Records Service.

Drinkwater's, his resignation is the remedy; if not, his retirement, which is required by his superior officers, is a mere sham and blind to cover more serious defects in the service. In other words, he is discharged to appease popular clamor and to prevent a popular verdict against the efficiency of the service itself."

The editorial infuriated J. W. Etheridge, superintendent of the Sixth District of the United States Life Saving Service and Drinkwater's immediate superior. Etheridge sent a copy of the editorial to Sumner I. Kimball, General Superintendent of the Life Saving Service, with a note reiterating his belief that Drinkwater was wrong, and charging that Drinkwater had put the newspaper up to writing the editorial. Wrote Etheridge: "Now this looks like he wanted to put the blame upon the Department. I am sure this is his work & his vindication."

The weather at Virginia Beach was wet and foggy on Monday, June 1, 1891, when Edward Drinkwater delivered the Seatack Life Saving Station and its property to his successor, William A. Payne.

After inspecting the premises, Payne observed in his log: "House apparently in good repair."

Edward Drinkwater and his wife Josephine and their large family lived in a small house adjacent to the Seatack Life Saving Station. Now that he was out of a job, Drinkwater was in need of money. He decided to sell a large tract of land he owned in Virginia Beach. On

April 28, 1891, he sold for four thousand dollars to the Seaside Hotel and Land Company, 116 acres of land, but reserving for himself the small family house and the site where stood the Seatack Life Saving Station. The first deed of the property Drinkwater bought in 1879 contained a clause permitting the Treasury Department to use part of the land for the Life Saving Station with the proviso that the land be returned to him when the Government no longer needed the land for life saving station purposes. Many years after his death, Drinkwater's heirs were to battle in the courts over the ownership of Edward's original property.

Edward Drinkwater died at his home in Virginia Beach on March 24, 1897, after a long illness. The funeral was conducted by the Reverend E. R. Savage at the Chapel by the Sea, a mission of the Eastern Shore Chapel. Located near the Dam Neck Mills Life Saving Station, the chapel was used by members of the Life Saving Service, many of whom had helped with the building. A large number of Drinkwater's old Seatack life saving crew attended the funeral.

Drinkwater was buried near Oceana, Virginia, on March 26, lacking but for one day the sixth anniversary of the tragic Dictator shipwreck.

Chapter Six

THE LEGEND

Over the years, the story of the Dictator shipwreck evolved into one of the most poignant legends in Virginia Beach. The fact that the Dictator's captain lost his wife and small child, and that the ship's figurehead stood at Sixteenth and oceanfront as a reminder of the tragedy, gave storytellers material on which to build a lasting emotional yarn.

The most familiar and popular legend, which is repeated even today, is that Captain Jorgensen never again returned to the sea, but each year until his death returned to Virginia Beach on March 27 to cast flowers on the water in memory of his family and crew.

It is also said that Jorgensen returned to the site of the figurehead, knelt in the sand in a silent prayer, placed red roses at the foot of the figurehead, then cast a bouquet of flowers into the sea. He then walked silently away.

Another account, also claiming that Jorgensen never returned to the sea, said he settled in Baltimore, Maryland, and annually, for thirty years, returned to the scene of the Dictator tragedy.

A different version contended that after the Dictator disaster, Jorgensen skippered a small ship along the East Coast, making Baltimore his homeport, and that he made annual pilgrimages to Virginia Beach.

It is interesting that few of the storytellers claimed that anyone had actually seen Captain Jorgensen place flowers near the figurehead or cast flowers on the sea. In most stories, Jorgensen appeared unnoticed.

As recent as 1976, a Norfolk magazine carried a story on the Dictator tragedy and related how the heartbroken Captain Jorgensen unnoticed returned each year" on the anniversary of the ill-fated event

Figurehead of the Dictator facing the Atlantic Ocean. Photo courtesy of The Mariners Museum, Newport News, Virginia.

to pay tribute to his beloved dead, adding that this continued for thirty-nine years. Having lived only twenty-six years beyond the 1891 shipwreck at Virginia Beach, Captain Jorgensen must have indeed returned "unnoticed."

During research for the Dictator story, contacts were made with several Virginia citizens who claimed that their ancestors were friends of Captain Jorgensen and that he had visited with them whenever he came to Virginia Beach, yet none could provide any proof or memorabilia of such meetings.

Several journalists for Norfolk newspapers exercised their imaginations to keep alive the legend of Captain Jorgensen.

One writer, who claimed to have spoken with Captain Jorgensen, wrote that the Dictator skipper never returned to sea, but that annually, for thirty years, he came to Virginia Beach to pray and throw flowers on the sea. When telling the same story again several years later, however, the same writer had forgotten some of his facts and changed the name of the Dictator's master to "Jarvensen."

One enterprising newspaper reporter decided in 1921 to stage an interview with one of the surfmen who was at the Seatack Life Saving Station at the time of the Dictator shipwreck. The surfman was in the Coast Guard and serving at the Virginia Beach Coast Guard Station which, in 1903, replaced the Seatack station.

The surfman related that he had spoken to Captain Jorgensen, who was the skipper of a new Norwegian tanker that had just arrived in Norfolk, enabling him to come to Virginia Beach to cast flowers on the waters in memory of his beloved family. Furthermore, Jorgensen's ship would call on Norfolk or Baltimore at least three times a year, allowing the captain to come to Norfolk to pay his respects to his wife and child buried in the Elmwood Cemetery.

It was an interesting story, but by then Captain Jorgensen had been dead for four years.

Jean Baptiste, the French sailor who remained with Mrs. Jorgensen until the Dictator's end, was also the subject of a romantic legend. He was treated as a hero and enigma. One story had it that Baptiste was not a Frenchman, but in reality an Austrian nobleman who, having been thrown aside as a court favorite, had cast his fortunes with those who serve before the mast.

Tales were told about the strong Baptiste attempting to swim ashore with Captain Jorgensen's wife tied to his back, when in fact both were washed overboard by strong seas, struggled separately and drowned. Baptiste was, of course, a hero. He chose to stay with Mrs. Jorgensen rather than try to save himself.

Legends are always interesting and fascinating, but unfortunately they often lack the important ingredient: truth.

CHAPTER SEVEN

A DEBT IS PAID

It was a dejected Jorgen Jorgensen who returned home to the island of Skaatoy in April 1891. It was spring, but in his sorrow for the loss of his family, his crew, and the gallant sailing ship Dictator, Jorgensen could not appreciate or see the splendor that was springtime in Norway.

The stigma of losing a ship is a scar that stays with sea captains as long as they live, even if the loss could not have been prevented. Although Captain Jorgensen had lost his ship under the most difficult conditions, and while no one blamed him for his actions, the Dictator master brooded for some time over his misfortune.

His employer in Moss, Christian M. Holst, owner of the Dictator, still confident that Jorgensen was a good leader and seaman, asked him to be master of the small, 489-ton bark Kirsten, which Holst had just acquired in 1891. Jorgensen declined the offer, saying he didn't want to return to sea for a while.

While contemplating his future, Jorgensen lived at the farmstead Donneviken, near the Donneviken inlet on the island of Skaatoy. He visited relatives and friends on the neighboring islands and in Kragero, where he met with old shipmates and pilots who brought the large sailing ships safely through the dangerous waters around the skerries.

During this nostalgic visit to Skaatoy Jorgensen decided to change his surname; henceforth he would be known as Donvig, a derivation of the word Donneviken.

One might think that he changed the surname as an attempt to shed the stigma of the Dictator loss that was associated with the name Jorgensen. This seems unlikely, however, because members of the maritime society have a close kinship to each other and are well acquainted with each other's personal lives. It would be impossible to hide one's problems behind another name.

In any event, it was and still is not unusual for Norwegians to elect to use the name of their farmstead or hometown when they move away from their place of birth. No official approval is needed for such action.

Although he didn't return to sea, Donvig remained active in maritime affairs, and in 1889, having moved to Christiania (now Oslo) after a stay in Horten, he joined with other shipmasters to form the Norwegian Shipmasters' Association.

But the tragic Dictator shipwreck was foremost in Donvig's mind. Deeply affected by the loss of life during the disaster, Donvig decided to develop a rescue apparatus that would save lives of those suffering ship sinkings in the future. He was to spend several years and most of his money on the life saving project.

The idea for his life saving device, he once wrote, came to him after he had viewed the Dictator wreckage strewn along the shore of Virginia Beach.

Among the debris of wreckage and floating timber, he found an undamaged water cask The cask, which had been stored inside the Dictator's poop, had floated free when the ship broke apart and was carried ashore by the sea. When the cask was retrieved, the small amount of water inside was found to be still fresh, free of any salt water.

If those aboard the Dictator had had a rescue apparatus constructed on the order of the water cask, they could have climbed into it and drifted safely ashore, protected against the surf and against being crushed by floating pieces of wreckage, Donvig wrote.

After several years of research and development with different types of rescue apparatus that would withstand the severest demands, Donvig announced in 1900 his new invention: "Captain Donvig's Life Saving Globe." He chose the English language for its title because English is a language used by all seafaring nations.

The apparatus, or buoy, was round as a globe, with a flattened bottom. Made from solid sheets of iron, the globe was 8 feet in diameter, 6½ feet high, with space to hold from 15 to 20 men. It weighed about two tons.

The globe had a flat double bottom divided into four tanks that had a total capacity of two hundred gallons of fresh water. This acted as ballast, and as each tank was emptied salt water was pumped in to take its place.

The interior was fitted with lockers for provisions and stores. The lockers were used as seats and had padded backs to preserve the occupants from injury. Access to the interior was made through three covered hatches.

Captain Jorgen M. Donvig stands beside his Life Saving Globe. Photo courtesy of Finn Krogsrud, Kragero, Norway.

In the center of the inner room was a funnel which could be shoved up, letting fresh air into the buoy. On the top were three small portholes, partly for the purpose of letting in light, but also for use in sending up rockets.

The buoy was provided with a moveable keel and a rudder which could be let down from the inside. Assisted by small oars, which were kept inside, the buoy could be propelled to land in fair weather.

On the outside of the buoy was a cork belt, on which the men could stand and row. The buoy was also supplied with an anchor and one hundred feet of steel rope and with sails, the air funnel serving as the mast.

Captain Donvig's Life Saving Globe was intended to be used from the decks of vessels. It could be released from the fastenings on the vessel by pulling a cord from the inside, allowing it to float off when the ship sank. Its form was intended to prevent it from being engulfed on the sinking of the vessel.

Demonstration of Captain Donvig's Life Saving Globe. Photo courtesy of Records of the Life Saving Service, National Archives and Records Service.

In promotional literature about his invention, Donvig noted that heavy surf had made it impossible to launch a lifeboat to rescue those stranded aboard the Dictator. Heavy surf and dangerous shoals would offer no problem for his rescue globe. It would come through undamaged, he contended.

There was considerable excitement in maritime circles about Captain Donvig's new rescue device, and good fortune seemed to be on his side. He exhibited the globe at the 1900 World Exposition in Paris, where he received a bronze medal in the life saving devices competition.

Donvig traveled throughout Europe demonstrating his rescue globe. He usually demonstrated the globe when the waves were running extremely high, in seas too rough for lifeboats to venture out safely.

Once, while a stiff easterly gale was raging in the English Channel, Donvig put on a demonstration for British shipping interests. Launched from a tug, which was almost swamped in the storm, Donvig's Life

Saving Globe rode over the waves like a cork and was remarkably steady.

After tossing about for fifteen minutes, Captain Donvig and one of his companions emerged from the inside of the globe, lashed themselves to the outside, set a small sail attached to the funnel, and then sailed the globe in a fairly direct course for several miles back to Dover Harbor.

Despite the implicit faith that he had in his device, and despite the many dramatic demonstrations he made before officials in Europe's maritime industries, Donvig was able to sell his invention to only one Norwegian shipowner.

While Captain Donvig's Life Saving Globe received many favorable comments in the press and maritime trade journals, the conservative shipowners were reluctant to try something as revolutionary as a floating rescue buoy. The lifeboat would remain their basic rescue apparatus. Sailors were reluctant to crawl into a steel chamber over which they would have little or no control. Furthermore, many of those who volunteered to let themselves be set adrift in the bobbing life saving globe suffered severe cases of seasickness.

Donvig tried to interest the American maritime community in his invention, but without success. Both the United States Life Saving Service and the Steamboat Inspection Service rejected the Donvig rescue apparatus.

Donvig suffered a bitter blow when even the Norwegian Life Saving Society turned thumbs down on his project. Still he continued to champion his cause, but money and energy ran out and he abandoned the life saving globe in 1906 after one last dramatic demonstration in the North Sea.

Donvig's invention was ahead of its time. Today his concept of a globed device for making rescue at sea is a reality. Self-propelled and unsinkable life saving capsules are now used to rescue workers from oil rigs and other types of offshore constructions. A new type lifeboat, shaped like a capsule and designed to be launched by free fall from the stern of a ship, has been developed by the Norwegian Ship Research Institute of the Directorate of Shipping.

Simultaneously with trying to market his life saving globe, Jorgen M. Donvig was also engaged in operating a shipping line. He became a shipowner in 1901 when he joined with Thorvald H. Davidsen to form the Donvig & Davidsen Shipping Line in Christiania.

Donvig and Davidsen purchased a steamship of 1,223 tons, which was built at Kockums Shipyard in Malmo, Sweden in 1882. They named it Bygdo, and used her as a tramp steamer in Scandinavian and European traffic.

In 1903 Donvig & Davidsen Shipping Line acquired the steamship Whydah, which they renamed Argo. The Argo, of 1,394 gross tons, was built in Flensburg, Germany, in 1884, and, like the Bygdo, was placed in tramp steamer trade.

The partnership broke up in 1904, with Davidsen forming his own one-ship company with the Bygdo. Donvig kept the Argo, which he continued to operate as a tramp steamer. His firm's name was Actieselskab Argo (Argo Corporation).

Running a shipping line is an expensive and risky business. To make money for its owners, a ship must always be on the go, her holds must be filled with cargo and her staterooms occupied with passengers. The turn-around in ports must be short, because an idle ship makes no money. Expenses can be enormous. Dock costs, fuel expenses, insurance fees, and salaries quickly add up to astronomical figures.

The tide was against Donvig's venture into the precarious shipping business, and his Argo shipping line folded in 1905. The Argo was sold to Japanese shipping interests.

There was, however, a bright moment in Jorgen M. Donvig's life. It overshadowed his failure with the life saving globe and the collapse of his ill-fated shipping business.

In 1904 he married forty-nine year old Antoinette Davidsen from Farsund, a small town on the southern tip of Norway. Donvig at this time was forty-five years old.

Jorgen Donvig's marriage to Antoinette Davidsen was to suffer financial problems. Having lost the money he had invested in his life saving globe, and failing to reap any profits from the shipping line, Donvig was teetering on the brink of financial ruin.

The sea, which had thrice failed him, was still to provide him with employment, not as an active partner in the adventures found beyond the waves on the horizon, but as a passive participant safely on shore.

Nearly broke, Donvig applied for and was accepted for a job in the Norwegian Lighthouse Service. On September 4, 1907, he became lighthouse keeper at Flatholmen, a small island off Tananger on the west coast of Norway, near Stavanger, which is famed for its many sardine-canning factories.

Work on the Flatholmen Lighthouse was routine and relatively simple. Donvig's main job was to see that the light's beacon was always lit, and that its lenses were polished and free of salt spray from the ocean. He gathered oil for the light, brought in firewood and food, and performed necessary station and housekeeping chores for Antoinette in their small quarters, adjacent to the lighthouse.

For a man who had always been active, full of vigor, and engaging in challenging pursuits, Donvig was to find the lighthouse job monotonous and uninspiring work. He became moody and withdrawn, brooding over his failures.

Antoinette tried to console him, seeking to convince him that the lighthouse job, albeit the small pay, was providing a vital service to the mariners who sailed near by in the North Sea. Why, some of his former shipmates may well have benefited from the guiding light he was responsible for.

After more than four years of inactivity at the Flatholmen Lighthouse, Jorgen Martinius Donvig could stand the monotonous routine no more. He resigned his post on January 31, 1912, and headed for the seaman's hiring halls.

He wanted to return to sea. But a big question gnawed on his mind. Who would hire an aging seaman who had failed so many times as he had in his chosen profession?

The weather was stormy on the morning of Friday, January 3, 1913, when the American steamer Julia Luckenbach, bound from Tampa to Baltimore with a cargo of phosphate rock, was creeping slowly through thick fog up the Chesapeake Bay. About 7:45 o'clock the steamer was about two miles south of the Tangier Sound Gas Buoy.

Suddenly, out of the dense fog, loomed the British tramp steamer Indrakuala, bound from Baltimore to New York. Before the bridge officers on the Julia Luckenbach could react, the bow of the Indrakuala had knifed into her starboard quarter, literally cutting the smaller American ship in two and crushing her forward compartments. Within two minutes, the Julia Luckenbach had sunk in fifty-two feet of water, leaving about twelve feet of her rigging and spars exposed to the stormy weather.

Damaged in the collision, the Indrakuala was beached by her master, about three miles away, in order to save the ship from the same fate which befell the Julia Luckenbach.

All those who were below decks on the Julia Luckenbach died in the disaster. Her master, Captain H. A. Gilbert, was sucked under and drowned as he tried to swim aft to rescue his wife Lillie, who was bedridden in their quarters.

Six of the Julia Luckenbach's crew were plucked out of the water by the Indrakuala, but one died of exposure shortly after being rescued. Altogether, fourteen persons died in the disaster.

Eight men were saved, and their rescue was as dramatic as the sinking.

When the Julia Luckenbach went under, ten crewmembers on deck scurried to safety in the rigging of the mainmast. Gale winds rocked the mast to and fro, and icy waves, whipped by the strong wind, froze the men.

One sailor, seeking a safer spot, tried to climb on the top of the smokestack and caught hold of the topping lift, but it broke away with the strain, tossing the luckless sailor to a watery grave.

The chief engineer, his hands bleeding from gripping the rope, became exhausted, let go his grip, and went down before anyone could help him.

The remaining eight sailors clung desperately to the rigging of the mainmast. One managed to lash himself to the mast. All the men suffered terribly from the chilling wind and icy water, which froze their clothing and benumbed their bodies.

At eleven o'clock, when they began to despair, the men sighted a ship coming down the bay. One man pulled out a red bandanna and waved it at the oncoming ship.

The ship was the 3,704-ton Danish steamship Pennsylvania, which was heading down the Chesapeake Bay from Baltimore. Her lookout had alerted her master, Captain J. E. Lessner, that a ship was in trouble as they approached the Tangier Island.

Captain Lessner directed the Pennsylvania toward the troubled ship, which was the Indrakuala. As the Pennsylvania neared the beached British steamer, the Indrakuala signaled for the Pennsylvania to rescue the men in the rigging of the Julia Luckenbach. The heavy fog almost precluded the Pennsylvania from seeing the masts of the Julia Luckenbach.

Captain Lessner directed his ship as close as he safely could toward the sunken Julia Luckenbach. The ship's whistle was blown to signal the shipwrecked sailors that help was on the way.

Then he turned to his first officer and said: "Mister Jorgensen. Let us rescue those poor sailors."

"Aye, aye, Sir," replied the first officer, whose full name was Jorgen Martinius Jorgensen Donvig.

So, finally, after a long and unproductive hiatus, Jorgensen Donvig had returned to sea, not as the master of his own ship, but as first officer, yet in a position of leadership and respect.

When he resigned his post as keeper of the Flatholmen Lighthouse, Donvig and his wife Antoinette moved to Christiania, where he made the rounds of hiring halls and shipping lines seeking employment.

Unsuccessful, he went to Copenhagen where he found the owners of The United Steamship Company (Det Forenede Dampskibsselkab) willing to offer him a job.

When he shipped out as first officer of the steamer Pennsylvania, he signed on as Jorgen Martinius Jorgensen. He employed the surnames Jorgensen and Donvig as they best suited his purposes.

Accepting Captain Lessner's order, Jorgensen, with four crewmen, climbed into a lifeboat and was lowered into the turbulent waters. Their launching, while successful, was made difficult by large waves washing over the Pennsylvania's deck.

Fighting a sea that was whipped to frenzy by a sixty mile an hour gale, Jorgensen steered while the four crewmen rowed the lifeboat toward the sunken Julia Luckenbach. Jorgensen and the oarsmen fought valiantly against the sea. Their boat nearly swamped several times. Twice they came between the protruding masts of the sunken ship, but each time they were carried away to windward.

Finally, after an hour of dogged persistency and in face of great danger, the Pennsylvania's lifeboat came close enough to the Julia Luckenbach's mainmast for Jorgensen to toss a line toward the sailors in the rigging. One sailor luckily caught the line with his foot, grabbed it and handed it to another who passed it around the mast and the backstay, and made it fast.

Jorgensen made his end of the line fast to the bow of the lifeboat, while shouting encouraging words to the shipwrecked sailors.

As the oarsmen tried to keep the lifeboat steady, Jorgensen began tossing a heaving line, to which was attached a ring life preserver, toward the sailors in the rigging. The sailors were to pull the line toward them, grab the ring life buoy, and then be pulled through the water into the lifeboat and safety by another line attached to the life buoy. This rescue operation was reminiscent of the time when Jorgensen wanted to have a boat pulled back and forth between the ship and shore during the Dictator shipwreck.

The rescue was not without difficulties. As Jorgensen tossed the line toward the mast, the wind would blow the heaving line away from the mast, and the line connecting the lifeboat to the mast had to be slackened frequently to prevent the lifeboat from swamping.

The powerful Jorgensen was relentless in tossing the heaving line against the strong wind toward the sailors in the mast. Whenever one of them grabbed the ring life preserver, Jorgensen and two of the oarsmen would quickly pull him to safety, while the other oarsmen kept the boat steady in the high-running sea.

After another hour of fighting the sea and the wind, Jorgensen and his crewmen had saved the eight sailors who had clung to the mast of the sunken Julia Luckenbach for nearly six hours.

The Julia Luckenbach sailors were half frozen and partially unconscious when the lifeboat was finally hoisted back on board the Pennsylvania. The shipwrecked sailors were received with stiff drams of brandy, wrapped in warm blankets, and given medical first aid.

When the shipwrecked sailors had rested and received warm food, they offered their gratitude and thanks to Captain Lessner for sending the ship's lifeboat to their rescue. Most of them believed they were near death when the Pennsylvania approached their sunken ship. While they had seen daring and bravery before, they told the captain they had never seen anything that could compare with that which First Officer Jorgensen displayed.

While Jorgensen considered the rescue as a duty not to be denied, his successful rescue effort in the Chesapeake Bay on January 3, 1913, must have seemed like a vindication of the Dictator tragedy which befell him off Virginia Beach nearly twenty-two years earlier.

He had made the complete circle.

He had come back.

A debt had been paid.

Among those who lauded Jorgensen for his heroism was the United States Government. The Consular Bureau of the Department of State recommended that Jorgensen be honored for aiding the distressed American seamen.

About a year after his rescue effort, the American Embassy in Copenhagen was to present him with a first class binocular glass bearing the following inscription: "From the President of the United States to Jorgen Jorgensen, First Officer of the Danish steamship Pennsylvania, in recognition of his heroic services in effecting the rescue at sea, on January 3, 1913, of eight members of the crew of the American steamship Julia Luckenbach."

After having rescued the Julie Luckenbach sailors, the Pennsylvania proceeded to Newport News. Due to the heavy seas and high winds, the ship did not dock until the next morning, on January 4. After the survivors had been taken ashore and Captain Lessner had made his report on the rescue to port officials, the Pennsylvania steamed out of Newport News on the morning of Sunday, January 5, bound for Copenhagen via Philadelphia.

As the Pennsylvania steamed out of Newport News, Jorgensen must have had mixed emotions about his second visit to the area.

Standing out of Hampton Roads he could see Norfolk, where his first wife Johanne Pauline and his son Carl Zealand were buried in Elmwood Cemetery. A little farther down the Chesapeake Bay, as the ship headed out into the Atlantic Ocean, was Virginia Beach, where one part of his life ended and another began. Perhaps there was a tear or two in his tired, blue eyes as he scanned the horizon, looking for what tomorrow would bring.

How ironic it was that none of those who perpetuated the legend of Captain Jorgensen—the story that he returned to Virginia Beach each year to honor those who lost their lives in the Dictator shipwreck—had recognized the true identity of the hero of the Julia Luckenbach rescue. The hero of their legend had indeed returned, but they had failed to see him. Instead they continued to repeat the romantic mythology.

Since the Pennsylvania was homeported in Copenhagen, Jorgensen Donvig decided that his wife should live in Denmark's capital city, and Antoinette moved to Copenhagen in 1914.

By August 1914, Europe was embroiled in World War I. While the Scandinavian countries—Norway, Denmark, and Sweden—were neutral, their shipping suffered serious curtailment and, in many cases, losses of ships and lives as the result of the war.

Jorgensen was again out of a job, and in 1916 he and Antoinette returned to Christiania where, as Captain Donvig, he began working at forming a company for constructing motor schooners. It was a good idea, but Donvig did not succeed in exploiting it. Today motor schooners are to be found in all waters throughout the world.

Antoinette succumbed to a long illness in the autumn of 1917. Donvig, despondent over his life's failures and himself suffering from ill health, died in Christiania on December 21, 1917.

Jorgensen Donvig's funeral was attended by many of his former shipmates and officials in the Norwegian maritime community. He had suffered many failures, but he was remembered as a man of strength and concern for his fellow man.

In an obituary, a Norwegian maritime magazine wrote: "Donvig was a special type of Norwegian seaman, active and courageous, an experienced ship master. He was a respected man, and many of his contemporaries will miss him as a good friend and comrade of bright humor, and as one who always had time to give good advice and a helping hand."

CHAPTER EIGHT

LOST AND FOUND

Hurricane Barbara, first observed during the night of August 11, 1953, northeast of the Bahamas, moved northward and struck the Carolina Capes between Morehead City and Ocracoke on August 13, then curved and swiped at Virginia Beach and Cape Henry early in the morning of August 14, inflicting heavy damage to waterfront property, downing trees and utility poles, tearing up shrubbery, and causing flooding and power failure along the shore from Virginia Beach to Willoughby Spit in Norfolk.

Among Virginia Beach property damaged by the hurricane was the priceless figurehead of the Norwegian bark Dictator. Since Emily Gregory first found the majestic figurehead near the Princess Anne Hotel sixty-two years earlier, it had stood at Sixteenth Street and the oceanfront, facing the Atlantic Ocean in memory of those who lost their lives on that fateful Good Friday of March 27, 1891. The buxom lady, strong as any seafaring lady could ever expect to be, had suffered much during her lonesome vigil; the sea and the weather had whipped her mercilessly, and unkind people, many of whom were tourists, not satisfied with admiring her beauty and grace, had carved and chipped pieces of wood from her frame for their souvenir collections.

Through the years, many attempts had been made to restore the worn figurehead, but each attempt suffered setbacks from the constant pounding of the sea, the rain, and the wind, and from the actions of thoughtless people. When Hurricane Barbara vented her fury on Virginia Beach, the figurehead was splintered badly, and city officials decided to remove it from its concrete foundation as a protection from more ravages of the weather and from further vandalism. The figurehead was wrapped in burlap and placed in the city's garage for safekeeping until such time as officials could find a method to treat and preserve the wooden statue.

When removal of the beloved landmark from its familiar stand caused concern among admiring Virginia Beach citizens, one city official, seeking to dispel their worry, noted that, "The figurehead from the Dictator is a part of Virginia Beach and we want to see that it remains with us forever."

Congressman Edward J. Robeson, whose district included Virginia Beach, made some inquiries with United States government agencies about the matter of restoring the figurehead, and in December 1953 Mrs. Maude C. Heys of Arlington, Virginia, sought out the Royal Norwegian Embassy in Washington, D.C., for assistance in having the figurehead restored and preserved for all time.

Mrs. Heys' interest in the figurehead was quite special and personal, since her father, James Burlas, was the surfman who found the body of Captain Jorgensen's son during an early morning patrol near the Princess Anne Hotel. After he left the Life Saving Service, Burlas changed his name to Burlasque and settled in Washington, where he became a groundskeeper at the White House.

After the initial flurry of interest in restoring the Dictator figurehead, the matter faded from the minds of public officials and citizens. Without any physical evidence to remind them of the wooden statue, all but a few people soon forgot about the figurehead, let alone the story of the Dictator shipwreck and the legend of Captain Jorgensen's annual pilgrimage to Virginia Beach.

The matter of restoring the Dictator figurehead was given no serious concern until September 1960, when Thomas Goode Baptist, an attorney in Washington, a resident of Arlington with a summer cottage in Virginia Beach, suggested such a restoration project when he visited with W. Russell Hatchett, City Manager of Virginia Beach. Hatchett thought it would be an interesting project, but left the initiative up to Baptist.

Later, Baptist related the story of the Dictator shipwreck and the tale of the deteriorated figurehead to Captain O. P. Aakenes, naval attaché at the Norwegian Embassy in Washington. Aakenes thought that he would have no trouble in getting the interest and support of the Association of Norwegian Shipbuilders to locate and provide a replacement for the Dictator figurehead. He urged Baptist to write an article about the Dictator and the figurehead for placement in a Norwegian maritime journal.

Thomas Goode Baptist. Photo by William O. Foss.

The enthused Baptist dashed off a letter to City Manager Hatchett, telling him the proposal of the Norwegian attaché, and offering the City of Virginia Beach his help in working out details for the figurehead replacement. Hatchett, warming to the opportunity, read Baptist's letter at an open meeting of the City Council, whose members expressed keen interest in the project.

It was then learned that the wooden figurehead was missing from its safekeeping spot in the city's garage. A thorough search was made in various other possible storage places, but to no avail. A theory developed that the figurehead had been buried by a city employee who didn't realize the significance of the wooden statue. Another theory had a city employee burning the figurehead. It is quite possible, of course, that someone knew very well of the importance of the figurehead, purloined it, and kept it for souvenir purposes or for possible future financial gain. One ought not to be surprised to one day hear news of the startling discovery of the long-missing Dictator figurehead!

Local Tidewater newspapers jumped on the "human interest" story, reviving the Dictator history, the Jorgensen legend, and the sad plight of the figurehead. A headline in the May 24, 1961 edition of

The Virginian-Pilot told its readers that "Beach Figurehead May Be Restored," with a teaser line noting "Norwegian Shipbuilders Interested." The next day, the Norfolk Ledger-Star reported that the "Gallant Pine Lady May Have Successor," with a teaser line suggesting her name as "Miss Dictator II."

Upon reading the Norfolk newspaper accounts, Thomas Baptist became a bit annoyed with City Manager Hatchett for releasing the story before contact had been made with any possible Norwegian sponsor. When Baptist related his predicament to Captain Aakenes, the Norwegian naval attaché laughed and said, "Well, Tom, now you'll have to sit down and write that article I've asked you to do for so long."

Calling his article, "The Story of a Norwegian Lady," Baptist related the fateful events of the Dictator disaster, the legend of Captain Jorgensen's thirty-year annual pilgrimage, and the story of the recovered figurehead, the "Wooden Lady embedded in a concrete base [who] for years kept a faithful watch over ships at sea while visitors and children around her would come and go unmindful of the tragedy and romance locked in her heart"

Ending his short article, Baptist, a romantic and sensitive man, wrote: "Through years of weather and deterioration we now observed that only the contour and the feet of the figurehead once carved from solid Norwegian pine, remained to mark the scene of this tragic human interest story.

"As our thoughts returned to the present, my daughters among many other questions asked: 'Why can't a Norwegian sister come to take her place? We miss our Norwegian Lady.'

"As we slowly walked up the beach I could not but think how a tragedy of yesteryear had created sympathetic understanding between people who never saw each other—though linked in history and tradition from the adventuring days of Leif Erickson to the present. How a Wooden Lady survivor of a bygone sea tragedy had become a symbol to perpetuate understanding and affect children born many generations after the tragedy.

"As a result of the Norwegian Lady's vigil on our Virginia Coastline, Norway has always seemed closer to Virginia Beach than to any other spot in America.

"City Fathers, including the Mayor, City Manager, Council, and townspeople alike would welcome a Norwegian Sister to take her place."

Captain Aakenes sent the article to the editor of Norsk Tidsskrift For Sjovesen (Norwegian Journal for Nautical Affairs), with a note saying that the article was an invitation to the Norwegian shipping industry to replace the Dictator figurehead in Virginia Beach. The Journal, published by the Naval Society at Horten, ran the article as written in English text in its September 1961 issue.

There was almost immediate positive reaction to the Baptist article.

Erik Bye, program producer for Radio Norway of the Norwegian Broadcasting Corporation, was in search of a good sea yam when he read Thomas Baptist's article. Fascinated by the story idea, Bye, who produces the radio and television show, Vi Gaar Ombord (We Go Aboard), met with Emil Andersen, Mayor of Moss, homeport of the Dictator, to discuss the possibility of the Norwegian Broadcasting Corporation and the City of Moss cooperating in a project aimed at giving the City of Virginia Beach a new Norwegian Lady, a bronze statue made by one of Norway's famous sculptors.

Emil Andersen, who had spent most of his adult life in politics and community work, was greatly enthused over the project At his suggestion, the project would be virtually an all-Moss affair, with the city's shipping firms and other industries conducting a fund drive to raise money for a statue to be erected in Virginia Beach, while two other groups, "The Jubilee Fund of 1920 for the Beautification of Moss City" (Moss was two hundred years old in 1920) and "The Society for the Welfare of the City of Moss" would raise funds to place a duplicate statue in Moss. The people of Moss were to raise more than fifty thousand Norwegian kroner for the two statues.

On December 10, 1961, Erik Bye dashed off a letter to Frank A. Dusch, Mayor of Virginia Beach, outlining the Norwegians' plan for giving the city a new Norwegian Lady. "I can at least promise a piece of sculpture that will be a thing of real beauty; something your city will be proud to have. And we would be proud to give it to you," wrote Bye.

Bye's love affair with the United States goes back to the end of World War II when he studied and received his BA degree from Midland College in Nebraska and later his MA from the University of Wisconsin. He has since made frequent trips to the United States, taping and filming radio and television shows for broadcast in Norway.

"Needless to say," replied Mayor Dusch, "it was with the greatest of pleasure to learn of the contributions being made and to such a great extent for purposes of erecting a new 'Norwegian Lady' in Virginia Beach."

Andersen and his Moss compatriots now commissioned fifty-four year old Ornulf Bast, one of Norway's leading sculptors, famed for his portrayal of young women, to create a statue that would be an appropriate replacement for the Dictator figurehead. Not only had he

Ornulf Bast, Norwegian sculptor, creator of the Norwegian Lady statue. Photo courtesy of Norsk Telegrambyraa A/S (Norwegian Telegraph Service), Oslo.

Close-up of clay model of the Norwegian Lady statue. Photo courtesy of Norsk Rikskringkasting (Norwegian Broadcasting Corporation), Oslo.

produced many statues and monuments with young women and girls as his central theme, but he had also established some kind of record for making figureheads that adorned the bows of numerous Norwegian ships. His work was popular in Norway and throughout Europe. A Norwegian art critic once wrote that Bast's sculptures of young women were made by a man in love.

On March 5, 1962, a winter storm of tremendous force began to lash the United States East Coast from Florida to New England. It lasted 5 days, killed 33 people, injured 1,252, and caused an estimated two hundred million dollars in property damage. Rampaging wind and water destroyed 1,793 dwellings, severely damaged 2,189, and lightly damaged 14,593.

This extra-tropical storm hit hard at Virginia Beach on March 7—Ash Wednesday—causing severe flooding conditions. Its violent tides pulled the supports out from under buildings, breaking many of them in half, carrying parts of the buildings and their furniture into the sea, or washing the debris along the flooded Atlantic and Pacific Avenues.

The storm ripped up a forty-foot stretch of the oceanfront seawall and completely demolished the wooden fishing pier at the

Bow section of the Dictator exposed by the Ash Wednesday storm in 1962. Now covered by sand, it lies about one hundred feet south of the end of Sixty-First Street in Virginia Beach. Photo by Professor Paul Saunier, Sr., Richmond, Virginia.

south end of Virginia Beach borough. Families were evacuated from their homes at Sandbridge up to the northern area of the mid-Sixty streets.

After the Ash Wednesday storm had subsided, many residents and sightseers walked along the waterfront of Virginia Beach to see the damage that the storm had done to the beach area.

Among the walkers were two friends, Professor Paul Saunier, Sr., an organist from Richmond, and retired Captain James R. Peake, Sr., then a Virginia Beach resident and member of the Virginia Pilot Association. Whenever they took their early morning beach walks together, the two men would observe the birds and small animals that lived near the shore. Professor Saunier once recorded his observations of the shore life in a booklet entitled, "Found at Virginia Beach." This time, however, while noting the storm's damage to marine life, such as thousands of seashells washed up on shore, their main interest was in two large pieces of wreckage that lay exposed near the foot of Sixtieth and Sixty-First Streets.

Saunier, who had a cottage nearby, became excited. For several years he had seen a few big timbers and iron spikes sticking up through the sand dunes. He theorized that the sand dunes hid the wreckage of the Dictator. Now he was convinced that the wreckage they had found was that of the Norwegian bark destroyed off Virginia Beach seventy-one years earlier.

The wreckage was in two pieces, one clearly identified as the bow section, the other as the stern section, with several of the stern posts still intact. Saunier and Peake paced off the sections which they thought were of the same ship, and they found each piece to be some ninety feet in length. The actual length of the Dictator was 191.4 feet. Saunier was convinced that they had found the Dictator wreckage, but Peake needed more proof.

How could the Dictator, which broke up near Fortieth Street, finally end up near Sixtieth Street, about a mile from the original grounding site?

Captain Peake checked the tidal current from the site of the Seatack Life Saving Station to Cape Henry, and found that these currents flow in a flood tide or northerly direction nearly ninety percent of the time. The current moves with great strength in a northeast gale when extreme high tides occur.

Peake presented their theory of the shifting Dictator wreckage to The Mariners Museum in Newport News, which confirmed that quite often ships would ground in one position and then be moved by another storm to a different location.

Still, Captain Peake and Professor Saunier carried their fact-finding search further. They carved pieces of wood from the wreckage and sent them to the United States Department of Agriculture's Forest Products Laboratory in Madison, Wisconsin, for analysis. The Laboratory reported that the wood samples were of pitched pine, tamarack, birch, and red oak.

A further check with the Saint John Shipbuilding Company revealed that the woods found in the wreckage were of the same types used to build ships in New Brunswick at the time when John Nevins constructed the full-rigger Connemara in 1867. The Connemara later became the Dictator.

Captain Peake and Professor Saunier finally agreed: The Dictator had been found!

It was a northeaster that destroyed the Dictator, and it was a northeaster that brought her wreckage ashore. But the Dictator was not to see the light of day for long. The beach property owner, annoyed over the throng of people who came to see the famous wreckage, had a bulldozer cover the remains of the Norwegian bark with sand. Over the years, the shifting sand has erased all visible signs of the tragic ship. Only memories remain.

CHAPTER NINE

THE NORWEGIAN LADY

In Virginia Beach it was eleven o'clock in the morning; in Moss it was five o'clock in the afternoon.

The day was Saturday, September 22, 1962.

The weather was remarkably similar in both cities—windy and chilly—but that didn't dampen the spirit and enthusiasm of their citizens as they met to unveil the duplicate copies of sculptor Ornulf Bast's latest work, The Norwegian Lady.

The nine-foot bronze statue, destined to be replacement for the missing Dictator figurehead in Virginia Beach, had left the Norwegian Naval Base at Horten, wrapped in heavy canvas and securely lashed to the deck on the naval training ship Haakon VII on July 31. Before the ship arrived with the Norwegian Lady at Pier 7 of the Norfolk Naval Base on September 4, she had been properly baptized in North Sea gales and made calls in the Shetland Islands, Rotterdam, and Bermuda, ports that had most likely been seen many times over by her predecessor.

A phalanx of politicians, civic leaders, and senior military officers, as well as the girls' drill team from the Princess Anne High School in Virginia Beach, were on hand to greet the Norwegian statue as it was gently' lowered by crane from the ship to the dock

Mills E. Godwin, Jr., Lieutenant Governor of Virginia, thanked Captain Knut E. Larsen, commanding officer of the Haakon VII, for bringing the statue to Virginia. He said, "This gesture on the part of the people of Moss, Norway, to the people of Virginia Beach, will further cement the strong ties of friendship that bind our two peoples."

A few days before the official unveiling ceremony, the Norwegian Lady and her granite pedestal were set in permanent place at a small area between the oceanfront and Twenty-Fifth Street. Her creator,

Royal Norwegian Navy training ship Haakon VII, which brought the Norwegian Lady statue to the United States. Photo courtesy of Norsk Telegrambyraa A/S (Norwegian Telegraph Service), Oslo.

sculptor Ornulf Bast, had come from his Oslo studio to supervise the placement.

Just as the statue was to be hoisted in place, Walter Lee Humphries, an assistant superintendent for the Virginia Beach Street Department, called on the crane operator to "wait a minute." He then got into a pickup truck and drove to Sixteenth Street and the oceanfront, where he used a crowbar to pry loose a piece of wood from the remnants of the base of the original Dictator figurehead. When he returned, one piece of the figurehead wood was placed under the base of the Norwegian Lady statue; the other was given as a memento to Ornulf Bast.

The sea was choppy and the wind was chilling the people who had come to see the unveiling of Ornulf Bast's Norwegian Lady statue and gift from the citizens of Moss to Virginia Beach. When Mrs. Anna Herland of Solund, a fishing village in western Norway, dressed in her colorful national costume, pulled the cord that unveiled the statue and presented it to Virginia Beach, the spectators were greeted to a majestic sight that warmed their hearts.

The towering nine-foot Norwegian Lady is a comely and buxom woman, clad in a vest and flowing dress of Norwegian tradition. Her left hand hangs limp at her side and her right hand is bent, clasping

Unveiling ceremony of the Norwegian Lady statue at Virginia Beach, September 22, 1962. At the microphone (left photo) are Navy Lieutenant Commander James A. Lovell, Jr., newly-selected American astronaut, and Erik Bye of the Norwegian Broadcasting Corporation. Next to Bye is Mrs. Anna Herland of Solund, Norway, who presented the statue to Virginia Beach, and Edward Drinkwater, son of the keeper of the Seatak Life Saving Station when the Dictator was wrecked off Virginia Beach on March 27, 1891. Simmons Photo Service photos for The Office of Public Information, City of Virginia Beach.

a lock of her shoulder-length hair. Her inspiring face and her eyes search the horizon as she looks longingly toward the Atlantic Ocean.

A plaque on the front of the statue states her mission:

I AM
THE NORWEGIAN LADY
I STAND HERE
AS MY SISTER BEFORE ME
TO WISH ALL MEN OF THE SEA
SAFE RETURN HOME

The American and Norwegian flags were raised simultaneously as the crowd applauded, and first graders from the W. T. Cooke Elementary School eagerly waved the little Norwegian flags they had made themselves.

It was a festive occasion, with Erik Bye conducting the unveiling ceremony. There were many speakers who, fortunately for the chilled crowd, made brief speeches. The Norwegian Ambassador to the United States, Paul Koht, spoke in both Norwegian and English, declaring that the statue was a symbol of the "viable and intimate ties" between Norway and the United

The Norwegian Lady in Virginia Beach, flanked by national flags of Norway and the United States. Photo by William O. Foss.

Norwegian Lady statue faces the Atlantic Ocean in Virginia Beach. Taylor Lewis & Associates Dockside Studio photo for the Department of Economic Development, Tourist Development Section, City of Virginia Beach.

States. "It is to the valiant seamen that this monument is erected." In accepting the statue, Virginia Beach Mayor Frank A. Dusch called the occasion "a milestone in the history of Virginia Beach."

The chopping sea prevented a fleet of boats from dropping memorial wreaths in the ocean; instead the wreaths were placed around the base of the statue, including one from Moss by its Vice Mayor Birger Eriksen.

Among the honored guests at the unveiling ceremony was Edward Drinkwater, whose father had been in charge of the Seatack Life Saving Station at the time of the Dictator shipwreck on March 27, 1891. The younger Edward, then eighteen years old, didn't actually see the Dictator break up, but driving his father's horse and wagon team, he later carried bodies of drowned victims from the beach to the railroad station for shipment to the Norfolk undertaker.

The second Edward Drinkwater became a member of the new life saving station that replaced the Seatack Life Saving Station in 1903. He retired from the United States Coast Guard as a Boatswain's Mate First Class.

The raising of the Norwegian Lady statue in both Moss and Virginia Beach could not have come about without the concerted contributions made by the people of Moss. Mayor Dusch recognized this united movement when, in his proclamation declaring September 22 as "Norwegian Lady Day," he observed that "the good people of Norway and particularly the town of Moss have demonstrated a deep affection for the people of Virginia Beach.

"These same Norwegian people have made a tremendous contribution to further cementing the strong ties that exist between the United States and Norway in the rebirth of the Norwegian Lady statue to replace the figurehead from the Norwegian bark, Dictator," said Mayor Dusch, adding that "this gesture has brought the people of Moss, Norway, and the people of Virginia Beach closer together through this magnificent demonstration of goodwill and friendship."

On the back of the Norwegian Lady statue, a plaque proclaims that "The people of Moss, Norway have sent me to commemorate Norwegian and American seamen who perished together when the Norwegian bark Dictator of Moss was wrecked off these shores on March 27th 1891."

Then follow the names of Moss business firms that donated funds and services toward bringing the statue to Virginia Beach. They are:

Aktieselskapet Alpha
A/S Asplund
Bjorn Bjornstand & Co.
Elektrokemisk A/S
Helly J. Hansen A/S
Sigurd Herlofson & Co. A/S
Il-O-Van Aluminiumvarerfabrik A/S
Kaare Mathisen
Moss Aktiemoller
A/S Moss Vaerft & Dokk
M. Peterson & Son A/S
Wilhelm Rosenvinge A/S
Vought & Holst
and
The Royal Norwegian Navy
The Norwegian Broadcasting Corp.

———————

With some forty statues already in the city, Moss has been called "the sculptors' city." Even so, the culture-minded citizens of Moss welcomed with great enthusiasm their newest statue, the Norwegian Lady.

Moss decided to place its Norwegian Lady statue near the City Hall Bridge running over the canal that divides the city's industrial center. As her sister in Virginia Beach faces east, the Moss statue faces west toward America. An array of beautiful red, white, and blue flowers decorates the base.

The canal area was decorated with American and Norwegian flags and with the city flag of Moss. As a remembrance of bygone days when Moss was homeport of great sailing ships, the Norwegian sail training ship Christian Radich was anchored nearby, her towering masts and rigging carrying all her colorful bunting. Also on hand for the festivities were the naval training ship Haakon VII, which had transported the sister statue to America, and the rescue boat Tonnes Puntervold.

Fredrik Schiorn, chairman of The Jubilee Fund of 1920 for the Beautification of Moss City, and W. Russell Hatchett, City Manager of Virginia Beach, jointly pulled the white tarpaulin that revealed the Norwegian Lady to the citizens of Moss as the Royal Norwegian Guard Regiment band played a fanfare.

The Norwegian Lady in Moss is surrounded by a beautiful flower garden and national flags of Norway and the United States. Photo courtesy of Arne Kinander, Moss.

To the citizens of Moss, the Norwegian Lady statue is considered not only a monument to those who lost their lives in the Dictator tragedy, but also as a memorial to all Moss seamen who ventured out to sea in the gallant sailing ships. In 1882 Moss was the homeport of seventy-five sailing ships that engaged in foreign trade; by 1907 the days of the sailing vessels were over and the last ship of the city's proud fleet of fullriggers, the Hovding (Chieftain), made her final cruise toward the yard to be cut up.

Consul Jorgen Herman Vogt, chairman of The Society for the Welfare of the City of Moss, the principal speaker, addressed his remarks to City Manager Hatchett and Clifton R. Wharton, the Ambassador of the United States to Norway, and other American guests, when he said: "The many visits of our ships to your great cities on the American Continent established a firm bond of friendship, which has flourished and progressed over the years. Now, today, we express the sincere wish that this long-established bond of friendship will continue to grow, and become firmer and closer.

"Between our Norwegian Lady in Moss and the Norwegian Lady in Virginia Beach, we have the great Atlantic Ocean—irresistible,

Moss Avis

Mandag 24. sept. 1962 · Løssalg 20 øre · Nr. 220 — 88. årg.

Avdukingen av Norwegian Lady

Her ser vi endel av de mest fremtredende blant gjester og vertskap under lørdagens avduking. Fra venstre: Fru Erik Bye, Mr. Russel Hatchett, konsul J. H. Vogt med frue, ordfører Emil Andersen og frue, rådmann Alf Herland, ambassadør Wharton og frue, admiral Hostvedt og frue, og nærmest vis disp. Schiørn. I bakgrunnen til venstre endel andre gjester.

Flere tusen mennesker strømmet til Kanalområdet i Moss lørdag ettermiddag for å overvære den høytidelige avduking av «The Norwegian Lady» — og selv om solen forsvant og det blåste surt fra sydvest — var det så meget som talte til følelsene at man ble varm, om hjertet i alle fall.

Igjen på netthinnen sitter bildet av Ørnulf Basts norske dame, den speidende, høyreiste sjømannshustru med det bekjende ansikt — en bronsestatue med blomster i rødt, hvitt og blått ved foten, en hyldest til sjøens folk.

På Rådhusbroen reist byflagget, som tross sitt lite maritime symbol, minnet om at høytideligheten var knyttet til byen — sjøfartsbyen Moss. Ved siden av smalt stjernebanneret friskt i vinden, og minnet om Virginia Beach, om mossebarkens forlis på Virginiakysten, som sytti år etter gav støtet til gaven til den fjerne, fremtidige vennskapsby. ...

Jo, det var meget som appellerte til vår følelser: Den hvite «Christian Radich» som lå fortøyet utenfor Helgerødstranden og bragte tanken hen på skuletiden, de arti seils dager i Moss. Det var også ekte flåtebesøk, bastante KNM «Haakon VII» ved Værlebryggen, nettopp hjemkommet etter turen over Atlanteren med lady'en, det var «Tønnes Punter vold» redningsskøyten — hva ligger det ikke av norsk sjømannshistorie bare i det ene ordet.

Og foran avdukings-høytideligheten: Stramme paraderende blakraver fra Sjømilitær Korps, HM Kongens Gardes Musikkorps med de stilige gallauniformer og med klingende spill, de friske karene fra Sjømannskoret, som har gledet oss så ofte før — ikke minst i radio — og så nasjonalsangene — folkelivet.

Ambassadørens tale

De forente staters ambassadør i Norge, Mr. Clifton R. Wharton, rettet sin tale til æresgjestene og «the generous people of Moss». — Det er for meg virkelig en stor glede å delta i denne høytidelighet i Moss idag, sa ambassadøren. — Den samme høytidelighet finner samtidig sted i Virginia Beach, USA.

Han minte om mossebarken «Dictator»s tragiske forlis utenfor Virginia Beach 27. mars 1891 da mange omkom, blant dem hustru og sønn til kapteinen Jørgensen. Selv om ulykken dengang var tragisk nok, har det sin egen historie blant de store tragedier. Likevel holdes minnet om forliset vedlike, og det knytter sammen, ikke bare folkene i Virginia Beach og Moss, men alle sjøfarende.

Den vakre utskårne marionettfigur fra «Dictator» ble reddet, og den ble satt opp i Virginia Beach som et minnesmerke over de som omkom. Gallionsfiguren sto, etter hva det fortelles, ved stranden i Virginia Beach, til den ble ødelagt i 1953 av orkanen «Barbara».

En norsk assisterende marineattaché ved ambassaden i Washington, som ofte besøkte Virginia Beach, skrev om den, og interessen ble vakt for det som fullføres idag, og som skyldes folk i Moss.

Ambassadøren dvelte ved hva The Norwegian Lady symboliserer: hyldesten til de norske sjømenn, som satte livet på havet, hyldesten til alle sjøfarende, og hyldesten til de uendelig tapre hustruer, som ventet og ventet på at deres menneskekjæreste fra havet skulle vende tilbake fra sjøen.

— Jeg vil først av alt få lov til å takke billedhuggeren, Ørnulf Bast, for den glimrende statue han har skapt — den norske sjømannshustru med den karakteristiske drakt — en statue i Moss og i USA, et symbol på vennskap mellom våre nasjoner.

— Jeg husker meget godt da Erik Bye for første gang kom til meg og ba meg delta i denne høytidelighet, sa ambassadøren. Jeg svarte at det ville jeg glede. Jeg er også glad for at vi ved denne anledning har en representant for Virginia Beach i Moss, city manager mr. Russel Hatchett. Ambassadør Clifton R. Wharton tegnet et vakkert bilde av Atlanterhavet, som både skiller og forener Norge og USA, og han minnet om at nu står en Norwegian Lady på begge sider av havet, den ene vendt mot øst, den annen mot vest.

— Atlanterhavet er den veien hele siden den ga sitt bidrag til menneskenes første kontakt. Atlanterhavet var også veien for de tusener og tusener av emigranter fra Norge til USA. Det er deres slektninger og venner — som har vært med til å bygge opp mitt store land, sa ambassadøren.

— Idag er jeg også glad for at Atlanterhavet også blir et bindeledd mellom våre land når det gjelder bestrebelsene for å opprettholde freden og fremme forståelse mellom hele verden. — Jeg er stolt

(Forts. s. 2)

Det første bildet av prinsesse Astrid m. P... datter, fotografert av NTB's Billedbyr...

Hovelsåsen kur ... totalskadet ved I

De 55 pasientene kom

Flisa: Verdier for over to millioner kroner gikk opp i flammer da Hovelsåsen kursted for alkohol ...

Kuvending i Ski skolestyre av Ap

Arbeiderpartiets skolestyregruppe i Ski gjorde i et ekstraordinært skolestyremøte lørdag helomvending i den meget omtalte «vaktmestersaken» og øyeblikkelig oppsto det under protester fra de øvrige skolestyremedlemmer, hadde trukket seg, angivelig på grunn av alle skriverier det uhellige oppstod omkring det famøse vedtaket.

Som kjent vedtok Arbeiderpartiet å ansette en mann fra Ski, en som hadde sitt medlemskap i partiet i orden, men som de faglige instanser overhodet ikke hadde tenkt på i sine innstillinger.

Normalt skal den som blir innstilt som nr. 2, rykke inn om

(høyre spalte delvis uleselig)

Farverik ramme om begivenheten i Moss

Ingen kald vind kunne hindre at det ble en festlig og høytidelig stund.

De innbudte gjester, gardemukken og sjømannskoret kom i prosesjon fra Rådhuset. Så fulgte æresgjestene, ambassadør Clifton R. Wharton med frue, city manager mr. Russel Hatchett, sjefen for Sjøforsvaret, admiral Erling Hostvedt, ordfører Emil Andersen med frue og fylkesmann Karl Hess Larsen med frue. I forreste rekke satt selvsagt også representanten for giverne og arrangøret, disponent Fr. Schiørn med frue og konsul J. H. Vogt med frue.

Gardemusikken spilte en marsj og deretter sang sjømannskoret, dirigent av Dag Christoffersen «Hav» av Oscar Borg.

Så talte disponent Fr. Schiørn, som ønsket alle velkommen og pekte på at felskabet til Moss Bys Vel og Jubileumsfondet av 1920 til Moss Bys Forskjønnelse var stolte og glade over at så mange ville være med og gjøre stunden til en verdifull fest for vår kjære by, Moss. Disponent Schiørn ønsket på engelsk æresgjestene hjertelig velkommen.

Sjømannskoret fremførte Bjørnstjerne Bjørnsons «Sjømannssang», som passet så

The Norwegian Lady er avduket av disp. Fr. Schiørn (t.h.) assistert av City Manager Russel Hatchett.

mystic, alluring, menacing—and at times without mercy—the ocean that parts us, and yet ties us together."

Ambassador Wharton said that the Norwegian Lady is a "tribute to the Norwegian seamen who lost their lives at sea, a tribute to all seafaring men and women, and a tribute to those noble and brave wives who wait and wait for their men to come home from the sea."

Noting the importance of the Atlantic Ocean and Norwegians to the growth of the United States, Ambassador Wharton told his audience "the Atlantic Ocean has been the road for thousands and thousands of emigrants from Norway to the United States of America. It was your ancestors and friends who helped to build my beloved country."

Virginia Beach and Moss, bound together by identical statues of the Norwegian Lady, both are dedicated to the sea, but in different manners. Virginia Beach, with a population of 236 thousand, makes its living from tourists, while Moss, with some twenty-five thousand inhabitants, is a shipping port that is growing in stature as an industrial city.

Virginia Beach is a young city; it didn't begin to grow into a community until about 1800. By 1906 it became an incorporated town, and a city of second class in 1952. Virginia Beach reached incorporated city status in 1963 when it annexed adjacent Princess Anne County.

Calling itself the World's Largest Resort City (270 square miles of commercial and agricultural area), Virginia Beach attracts over a million and a half tourists annually. They swim and sail in the Atlantic Ocean, play on the white beaches, and sightsee nearby historical landmarks.

Moss became a city in 1720, but it has been a small seaport town since 1500. Located midway on the beautiful Oslofjord, it is the central point of both overland and ocean traffic. With excellent port facilities, including a modern roll-on/roll-off dock, Moss has a lively and profitable shipping trade. Ferries between Horten and Moss enable the city to reap the benefits of the heavy auto traffic between Norway and the European Continent.

The Moss newspaper, Moss Avis, aptly characterized the importance of the unveiling of the Norwegian Lady statues in Moss and Virginia Beach in an editorial: "This is no big international event. Hardly. But it is a meeting of the hearts of cities on two continents, between their representatives, and thus between the citizens of those cities. A bond has been made for the future.

"Each bond which is made across the borders, over the ocean, between people in different countries, individually and collectively, is a commitment to peace."

While the Norwegian Lady statues joined Moss and Virginia Beach as sister cities, it was not until 1974 that the Virginia Beach City Council adopted a resolution officially extending an invitation to Moss to participate with it as a sister city "for the purpose of creating greater mutual understanding between the people of our two great cities and nations." The Board of Aldermen of the City of Moss unanimously resolved to accept the invitation for the social and cultural affiliation.

———————

When W. Russell Hatchett, City Manager of Virginia Beach, arrived in Moss for the unveiling of the Norwegian Lady statue, he presented the Mayor of Moss, Emil Andersen, with a letter from the Ladies Auxiliary to the Virginia Beach Borough Volunteer Fire Department pledging that the Auxiliary would place a wreath at the base of the statue at Twenty-Fifth Street and oceanfront each year in memory of those who perished in the Dictator sinking.

The ladies have been true to their word. On each anniversary of the Dictator tragedy—either on the actual date of the shipwreck, March 27, or the nearest Saturday (to enable the city's school children to participate)—the Auxiliary stages a brief but solemn ceremony at the Norwegian Lady statue.

The ladies of the Auxiliary strive to have a visiting Norwegian as honored guest at the ceremonies. In 1963, Miss Ann-Kristin Olsen from Kristiansand, an exchange student attending Princess Anne High School in Virginia Beach, was the guest of honor. Queen Azalea XIII of the annual Norfolk Azalea Festival, Miss Kari Borten, was so honored in 1966. Royal Norwegian Navy Captain K. Tholffen represented Moss in the 1971 ceremonies.

Brief remarks are made by local officials; the history of the Dictator is read by the Auxiliary historian, and, as he has done since the inception of the annual event, Rolf Williams, the Norwegian Consul in Norfolk, reminds the audience of the importance of the historical and cultural ties that the Norwegian Lady statue brings to the people of Moss and Virginia Beach.

After the ladies have placed a wreath at the foot of the statue, the Auxiliary president and her aides remove the wreath and a boat (at first in the First Department's own rescue boat, lately in an Army landing craft), heads out on the Atlantic Ocean several hundred yards

Beverly Hicks, the 1968 president of the Ladies Auxiliary to the Virginia Beach Borough Volunteer Fire Department, with Jenny Penner and Celia Morse, gets ready to toss a memorial wreath into the sea from an Army landing craft. Photo courtesy of Ladies Auxiliary to the Virginia Beach Borough Volunteer Fire Department.

away from the shore, and casts the wreath upon the sea, keeping alive the poignant legend of Captain Jorgensen.

A few times, when rough weather prevented the ladies from venturing out to sea, the ceremony was completed by tossing the flowers on the waters from the beach.

While the Ladies Auxiliary to the Virginia Beach Borough Volunteer Fire Department honored their pledge to the City of Moss, officials in Virginia Beach soon forgot about the promise they made to the generous citizens of Moss, that of providing the Norwegian Lady with a "lovely park."

The location of the Norwegian Lady statue, while central to tourist activities, could hardly be called an appropriate setting for a work of art. On her sides were the bleak end walls of the Holiday Inn and the Princess Anne Inn, while behind her was an automobile parking lot. In front of the statue was the boardwalk and nature's own artwork, the Atlantic Ocean.

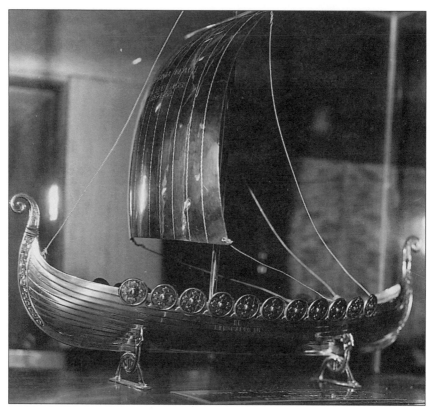

Silver Viking ship presented to Virginia Beach by the city of Moss, Norway. The replica is on display at The Old Coast Guard Station. Photo by William O. Foss.

In 1972, the tenth anniversary of the arrival of the Norwegian Lady statue in Virginia Beach, the weekly newspaper, Virginia Beach Sun, attempted to drum up support for a public fund to build the park which city officials had forgotten about. The Sun's appeal for funds for the Norwegian Lady Park fell on unsympathetic ears. "How sad that the American people cannot equal the generosity of their Norwegian friends," wrote the paper's editor.

It should be noted that not only did the city of Moss honor Virginia Beach with a beautiful statue, but when City Manager Hatchett returned from Moss, he brought with him another gift, a handsome sterling silver replica of a Viking ship. The Moss Viking ship is now on display in the Virginia Beach City Manager's office. Virginia Beach's gifts to Moss appear to have been in the form of city flags, emblems, and similar paraphernalia.

There were others, and especially the Norwegian Consul Rolf Williams and Thomas G. Baptist, who reminded Virginia Beach city officials of their promise to beautify the area around the Norwegian Lady statue.

Baptist bombarded the City Manager's office with letters and proposals for constructing a park, and he solicited the support of many community leaders, including members of the Hampton Roads branch of the Sons of Norway lodge.

Finally, in 1974, Virginia Beach began its Norwegian Lady improvement project to beautify the area around the statue. The city set aside twenty-thousand dollars for the lighting, utilities, and landscaping material, but by the time the project was completed in 1975, the total project cost had risen to over forty-two thousand dollars. The two Norwegian Lady statues together cost Norwegian fundraisers fifty-thousand Norwegian kroner, or about 7,125 dollars in American currency in 1962! But the Norwegian Lady in Virginia Beach now stands in the center of a handsome mall, well in keeping with her artistic splendor.

A dreamer and a doer, Thomas Baptist got together with several civic leaders interested in perpetuating the Norwegian Lady image, and in October 1973 they formed the Norwegian Lady Plaza Foundation, a non-profit corporation.

Baptist became the Foundation's president, while former mayor of Virginia Beach Donald H. Rhodes was named its secretary. Other members of the initial board of trustees were Rolf Williams, T. Johan Lassen, Lawrence R. Luhring, Albin R. Mailhes, and Robert H. Callis.

One of the Foundation's aims was to construct a plaza surrounding the site of the Norwegian Lady statue, and Baptist announced plans to raise two hundred thousand dollars to finance the construction of a display area for relics of the Dictator, art and handicraft from Norway, and artifacts and memorabilia of Norwegian emigrants to the United States.

The Foundation also pledged itself to foster the continuation of the traditional good will existing between the United States and Norway, and "to strive for public preservation of all elements of the legend of the Norwegian Lady including Norwegian heritage, cultural, social, and historical aspects."

In 1976 the Norwegian Lady Plaza Foundation launched its first annual Norwegian Lady Exchange Program in which female high school students from Moss and Virginia Beach would exchange visits to each other's homes and cities for a two-week period during the summer months. The program received support and cooperation from the Virginia Beach City Council, the Virginia Beach Chamber of Commerce, and other civic-minded organizations. The Foundation raised funds for the project from various businesses and private sources.

Ruth Anne Aas from the Jeloy section of Moss was named the Norwegian Lady from Moss, while Lee Ann Foster from Kempsville High School was selected as the Norwegian Lady from Virginia Beach. During their two week stay in each other's home city, the girls enjoyed a variety of entertainment and activities, including meetings with city officials and youth groups, helicopter flights and boat rides, tours of historical landmarks, and a visit to their national capitals.

In recent years, the Norwegian Lady statue has become the focal point of civic activities in Virginia Beach. It is the scene of public concerts, the site for children's art and puppet shows, the reviewing stand for the Boardwalk Easter Parade, the starting and ending point for the Shamrock Marathon race, a featured landmark to be seen by visiting dignitaries and tourists, and the center of activities during the annual Virginia Beach Neptune Festival.

To some, the Norwegian Lady is a favorite site for a rendezvous, to others it is a shrine, a place for silent meditation to honor the hardy seamen of the windjammer era who gave their lives and whose deeds charted the course for everlasting friendship and mutual respect between the United States of America and the Kingdom of Norway.

CHAPTER TEN

THE STORY CONTINUES

[History is alive. History never ends. It goes on forever and is continuously revised—updated with new information and new characters that brings the stories alive to newer generations. The story of The Norwegian Lady, which began with the tragic wreck of the Norwegian bark Dictator on March 27, 1891, continues to unfold today with new players from both Norway and America, especially those who keep alive the cultural ties between the citizens of Moss and Virginia Beach.]

When the Norwegian Lady statue was erected in September 1962, the Ladies Auxiliary of the Virginia Beach Borough Volunteer Fire Department pledged that the Auxiliary would conduct an annual ceremony to honor those who perished in the Dictator sinking.

The ladies have kept their promise. On each anniversary of the Dictator tragedy, either on March 27, the actual date of the shipwreck, or the nearest Saturday, the ladies of the Auxiliary, stages a solemn ceremony at the Norwegian Lady statue.

Attendance at the Dictator memorial ceremony has been on the increase as more people are becoming aware of its historic and cultural significance. Speakers at the event include the mayor of Virginia Beach and other dignitaries, often a Norwegian official.

Virginia Beach Mayor Meyera E. Oberndorf continues the tradition of telling the audience the history of the Dictator shipwreck and rescue effort. The Navy's Atlantic Fleet Band plays at the

Norwegian-Americans and their friends celebrate May 17th, Norway's Constitution Day, at the Norwegian Lady statue in Virginia Beach. Rolf A. Williams, Norwegian Consul for Norway in Virginia, speaks at the 2002 ceremony, whose attendees included members of the Hampton Roads Sons of Norway Lodge No. 522. Photo by William O. Foss

ceremony, and firemen from the Virginia Beach Fire Department raise the American and Norwegian flags up the flagstaffs by the Norwegian Lady statue. Traditionally the ceremony ends with the casting of a floral wreath upon the waters of the Atlantic Ocean.

While their membership has dwindled over the years, the few remaining volunteers of the Ladies Auxiliary continue to perform their annual ritual honoring the lost Norwegian sailors.

In recent years the Auxiliary volunteers have been joined in their annual remembrance of the Dictator tragedy by members of the Sons of Norway, Hampton Roads Lodge No. 522. Lodge members also rally around the Norwegian lady statue on May 17 to celebrate Norway's constitution day.

Near the Norwegian Lady statue, at 24th Street and Atlantic Avenue, stands The Old Coast Guard Station, a descendant of the Seatack Life Saving Station, whose crew rescued the Dictator survivors. Now a nautical museum, The Old Coast Guard Station gives visitors a rare insight into the early days of shipwrecks and life-saving efforts. Among its many interesting exhibits are artifacts from the Norwegian bark Dictator. The museum's store offers nautical items, books, and works from local artists.

Due to its historic ties to the Dictator shipwreck, The Old Coast Guard Station is an active participant in the annual Dictator memorial event. The museum opens its doors and welcomes visitors to enjoy its hospitality and view the Dictator artifacts exhibit as well as other marine life-saving displays.

The Old Coast Guard Station, which was built in 1903 as Virginia Beach Life-Saving Station No. 2, became a United States Coast Guard Station in 1915. The station had a long and illustrious history which ended in 1969 when it was decommissioned by the Coast Guard.

After sitting empty for ten years, the old building was destined for demolition in 1979, but a group of concerned citizens rallied public support and financially saved it from destruction.

The Virginia Beach Maritime Museum was established in 1979 as a private non-profit foundation dedicated to the presentation and preservation of Virginia maritime history and artifacts. In 1988 the name was changed to The Old Coast Guard Station. The station is a Virginia Historic Landmark and is listed on the National Register of Historic Places.

Near the Norwegian Lady Statue in Virginia Beach, stands The Old Coast Guard Station, a descendant of the Seatack Life Saving Station, whose crew rescued the Dictator survivors in 1891. Now a nautical museum, the station gives visitors a rare insight into the early days of shipwrecks and life-saving efforts. Among its many interesting exhibits are artifacts from the Norwegian bark Dictator. Photo courtesy The Old Coast Guard Station, Virginia Beach.

STORY TELLING

History comes alive around the Norwegian Lady statue during the evening hours of the summer months when a storyteller dramatically narrates the tragic events of the Dictator shipwreck.

Tourists and local residents strolling on the beach and boardwalk are invited to sit on the grass or chairs behind the statue and hear the true story of the 1891 shipwreck. A seasoned storyteller, costumed as a 19th century seaman, using a few key props, special lighting and sound effects, thrills the audience with his dramatic rendition of the life and death struggle of the Dictator crew.

"The Wreck of the Dictator," one-man play, sponsored by the city of Virginia Beach, was written and produced by Gary Spell, who starred in the initial 2000 show. Derek Leonidoff was the featured actor in the 2001 production.

The play continues to be part of the city's effort to promote local history.

Other entertainers have presented their versions of the Dictator story. Husband and wife team, Bentley Anderson and Shirley Hurd, have given dramatic readings at various places, including the Contemporary Art Center of Virginia Beach.

HANDS ACROSS THE SEA

While the impressive-looking Norwegian Lady statue memorializes those who lost their lives in the Dictator shipwreck, it also symbolizes the sister city arrangement between Moss, Norway, and Virginia Beach. In 1974, the Virginia Beach City Council adopted a resolution extending an invitation to Moss to become a sister city for the purpose of creating greater mutual understanding between the people of Moss and Virginia Beach. The Council of Aldermen of the city of Moss unanimously accepted the invitation.

The Moss-Virginia Beach Sister City Foundation was formed to encourage more cultural relationship between the two cities. The results have been a steady increase in across the sea contacts between both official and private groups, as well as individual travelers.

In 1990, for example, the Moss Skolemusikkorps (School Band),

Queen Sonja of Norway (dressed in black and wearing glasses) paid homage to the Dictator victims when she placed a floral bouquet at the base of the Norwegian Lady Statue in Virginia Beach on October 13, 1995. Among those who attended the ceremony were Norwegian immigrants who were introduced to the queen. Photo courtesy of Carole J. Arnold, City Photographer, Virginia Beach.

celebrated their 80th birthday by visiting Virginia Beach. Virginia Beach Mayor Meyera Oberndorf went to Norway in 1995 to help celebrate the 275th anniversary of the city of Moss. While Mayor of Moss, Bjorn Barang, a Sons of Norway member, made several visits to Virginia Beach.

In October 1995, King Harald and Queen Sonja of Norway visited Hampton Roads. While the king attended functions at the North Atlantic Treaty Organization (NATO) naval headquarters in Norfolk, Queen Sonja visited Virginia Beach. She went to the oceanfront where she placed a floral bouquet at the base of the Norwegian Lady statue to commemorate the Dictator tragedy and ties between the two sister cities - Virginia Beach and Moss. A happy crowd welcomed the stately queen, who shook hands and engaged in brief conversation with the onlookers, some who were Norwegian immigrants wearing their Norwegian national costumes.

In Moss, which is well known for its many sculptures, the Norwegian Lady statue has become one of the city's most famous attractions. In April 1991 the Moss Norwegian Lady statue was removed from its original place by the Town Hall Bridge to a charming park alongside the Canal and Moss Sound, a most appropriate site for a lady of the sea.

FINAL HONOR

Thomas Goode Baptist, the man directly responsible for getting the Norwegian Lady statue erected in Virginia Beach, died on February 3, 1993. His enthusiasm and persistence to honor the Dictator victims with a special monument stirred the interest of seafaring folks on both sides of the Atlantic Ocean, culminating in the citizens of Moss contributing funds to erect a majestic statue in Virginia Beach, but also raise a duplicate memorial in their own city, the homeport of the wrecked Dictator.

Following the Dictator tragedy, Captain Jorgen Jorgensen became a pioneer in marine lifesaving. He spent much of his time and money developing the state of art in marine lifesaving. His major accomplishment was development of the Donvig Globe. The concepts he initiated are today being used worldwide on offshore oil rigs in the form of survival capsules.

Baptist felt that Captain Jorgensen should be honored for his marine lifesaving efforts and set out to get the United States Coast Guard to officially recognize his Norwegian hero's safety work.

Baptist's campaign came to fruition when, in September 1981, the U.S. Coast Guard posthumously awarded Captain Jorgensen a certificate of public service commendation for his pioneering work in marine lifesaving equipment.

The Coast Guard award to Captain Jorgensen is on display in the Dictator exhibit at The Old Coast Guard Station in Virginia Beach.

EPILOGUE

Since history is a continuing process of recording human events, I am ending this tale with the journalistic phrase, "More To Come."

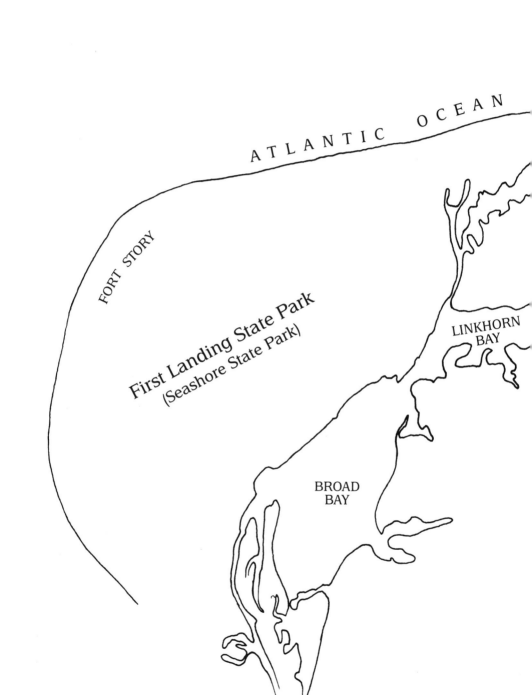

Norwegian Lady Statue and Park

Norwegian Lady Figurehead

Princess Anne Hotel

BOSTON

NEW YORK
PHILADELPHIA

WASHINGTON

RICHMOND

VIRGINIA BEACH

SAVANNAH

MIAMI

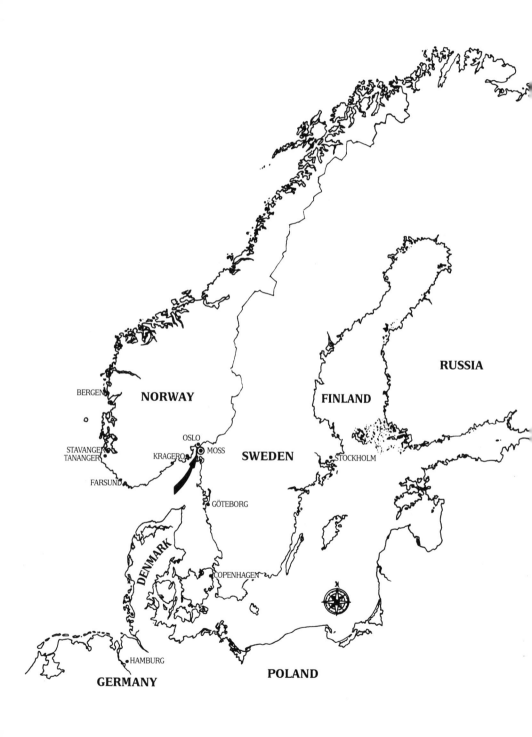

ACKNOWLEDGMENTS

I wish to extend my gratitude to the many persons who gave me every possible assistance in my search for material for a history that required the author to seek out information in four countries.

My major contributors of historical data are:

UNITED STATES OF AMERICA

Dorothy L Atwater, Virginia Beach
Thomas Goode Baptist, Arlington
Vernon Drinkwater, Sr., Virginia Beach
Carolyn G. Gray, Virginia Beach
William F. Hampshire, Norfolk
W. Russell Hatchett, Virginia Beach
Charles H. Hoffman, Norfolk
Cornelia R. Holland, Virginia Beach
Mrs. Walton Holland, Virginia Beach
Walter Lee Humphries, Virginia Beach
Mrs. Frank Klepper, Norfolk
Captain James R. Peake, Sr., Norfolk
Professor Paul Saunier, Sr., Richmond
Bayside Branch, Virginia Beach Public Libraries
Central Files, City of Virginia Beach
Department of Economic Development, Tourist Development
    Section, City of Virginia Beach
Office of Public Information, City of Virginia Beach
Sargeant Memorial Room, Kirn Memorial Library, Norfolk
Virginia State Library, Richmond
The Mariners Museum, Newport News
National Archives and Records Service, Washington, D.C.
National Weather Service Office, Norfolk

Public Affairs Division, United States Coast Guard, Washington, D.C.

Public Affairs Office, Fifth Coast Guard District, Portsmouth

Norwegian Information Service in the United States, New York

NORWAY

Arne Kinander, Moss

Finn Krogsrud, Kragero

Johanne Marie Kvam, Kragero

Emil W. Martens, Moss

Rino Thorne, Moss

Jorgen Herman Vogt, Moss

Det Konglige Norske Utenriksdepartment (Royal Norwegian Foreign Affairs Department), Oslo

Embassy of the United States of America, Oslo

Kystdirektoratet, Fyravdelingen (Coastal Directorate, Lighthouse Section), Oslo

Norsk Rikskringkasting (Norwegian Broadcasting Corporation), Oslo

Norsk Sjofartsmuseum (Norwegian Maritime Museum), Oslo

Norsk Skibsforerforbund (Norwegian Shipmasters' Association), Oslo

Universitetsbiblioteket i Oslo (Library, University of Oslo)

CANADA

Public Archives of Canada, Ottawa

Provincial Archives, New Brunswick, Fredricton

ENGLAND

Lloyd's, London

National Maritime Museum, Greenwich

BIBLIOGRAPHY

PUBLICATIONS

Many interesting items were found in various editions of the following publications:

The Daily Press, Newport News
The Ledger Dispatch, Norfolk
The New Daily Pilot, Norfolk
New Norfolk, Norfolk
New York Evening Post, New York
The New York Times, New York
The Norfolk Landmark, Norfolk
Norwegian American Commerce, New York
The Public Ledger, Norfolk
Virginia Beach Beacon, Virginia Beach
Virginia Beach Sun, Virginia Beach
Virginia Beach Sun-News, Virginia Beach
The Virginian-Pilot, Norfolk
Kragero Blad, Kragero
Moss Avis, Moss
Moss Dagblad, Moss
Norges Handels og Sjofartstidende, Oslo
Norges Skibforertidende, Oslo
Norsk Tidsskrift for Sjovesen, Horten
Lloyd's Weekly Shipping Index, London

BOOKS

Burgess, Robert H., *Chesapeake Circle*, Cornell Maritime Press, Inc., Cambridge, Md., 1965.

Edmunds, Pocahontas Wight, *Tales of the Virginia Coast*, The Dietz Press, Richmond, Va., 1950.

Ferebe, E. E. & Wilson, J. Pendleton *Jr., An Economic and Social Survey of Princess Anne County,* University of Virginia, 1924.

Jordan, James M. & Frederick &, Virginia Beach-A Pictorial History, Thomas F. Hale, 1974.

Kyle, Louisa Venable, *The History of Eastern Shore Chapel and Lynnhaven Parish 1642-1969,* printed by Teagle & Little, Inc., Norfolk, Va., 1969.

Norske Seilskibsrederler Gjennem 50 Aar, Fredhois Forlag A/S., Oslo, Norway.

Parmann, Oistein, *Norsk Skulptur I Femti Aar,* Dreyer, Oslo, Norway.

Sandberg, Bjorn, *En Vandring I Det Gamle Kragero,* Berg-Kragero Museum, Kragero, Norway, 1965.

Whichard, Rogers Dey, Editor, *The History of Lower Tidewater Virginia,* Volume II, Lewis Historical Publishing Co., Inc., New York, 1959.

Worm-Muller, Dr. Jac. S., Redaktor, *Den Norske Sjofartshistorie,* Bind III, Steenske Forlag, Oslo, Norway, 1929.

ALSO

VARIOUS EDITIONS OF THE FOLLOWING ANNUALS:

Annual Reports of the Operations of the United States Life Saving Service, Washington, D.C.

Records of American and Foreign Shipping, American Shipmasters' Association, New York

Lloyd's Register, London.

Den Norske Veritas Register Over Norske Skibe, Christiania (Oslo).

INDEX